766

1863   1941

M. Ussishkin

MENAHEM USSISHKIN
HIS LIFE AND WORK

By
DR. JOSEPH KLAUSNER
*Professor at the Hebrew University,
Jerusalem.*

SCOPUS PUBLISHING COMPANY
NEW YORK   1942

COPYRIGHT BY
SCOPUS PUBLISHING COMPANY
NEW YORK, N. Y.
1942

F/P/W
Printed in the United States of America

PUBLISHER'S NOTE

THE PUBLISHERS ACKNOWLEDGE APPRECIATION TO MR. I. M. LASK OF JERUSALEM, WHO TRANSLATED THE VOLUME FROM HEBREW; TO MISS SULAMITH SCHWARTZ, WHO EDITED THE MANUSRIPT; TO MR. ELIAS M. EPSTEIN OF THE HEAD OFFICE OF THE JEWISH NATIONAL FUND IN JERUSALEM, WHO WAS MOST HELPFUL IN THE PREPARATION OF THE MATERIAL; AND TO MR. MENDEL N. FISHER, EXECUTIVE DIRECTOR OF THE JEWISH NATIONAL FUND OF AMERICA, WHOSE GUIDANCE AND SUPERVISION HAS MADE POSSIBLE THE PUBLICATION OF THIS VOLUME.

CONTENTS

	Preface	7
	Introduction	13
I	Childhood and Youth	15
II	Work in the Movement Begins	25
III	The First Journey to the Land of Israel	33
IV	The Beginnings of Political Zionism	43
V	The Minsk Conference	51
VI	Organizing the Yishuv	55
VII	The Uganda Conflict	65
VIII	"Our Program"	75
IX	The Russian and Turkish Revolutions	85
X	The Language Conflict in Palestine	99
XI	1914-1918	103
XII	With the Zionist Delegation in Palestine	115
XIII	The Redemption of Emek Jezreel	121
XIV	Chairman of the Jewish National Fund	127
XV	The Partition Issue	135
XVI	The Last Days	141
XVII	Man and Leader	149

Preface

EVERY PERSONALITY HAS ITS KEY CHARACTERISTIC. Once grasped, the key provides access not only to the main compartments of mood and thought, inclination, will and action, which appear in the public record of a man's life. It provides access also to the screened chambers of his inner self, where causes are caused, where pros and cons are weighed in the delicate scales of introspection, where diverse impulses are often in conflict before the ultimate direction is determined, where the iron will is forged in tormenting flames of passion, ambition and purpose. This source of causes does not usually appear on the surface but is nonetheless a telling factor in the story. The key which unlocks the enigma of personality, opens the door to this source as well.

All who knew Menahem Ussishkin will agree that integrity was his key characteristic.

Integrity is not a monolithic word. It has varied aspects and angles. Honesty of purpose and fothrightness are its main components. Yet it is more than these. Consistency, too, is a phase of integrity. There is, moreover, a structural aspect of integrity. It is manifested in the architecture of an edifice, just as of a movement or a personality. Integrity in the sense of wholeness and harmony gives symmetry and proportion to the constituent

One need not indulge in Ussishkin-olatry to recognize the integrity which characterized the man's actions and character, *Toho Kebaro*. His wisdom was not of the subtle kind, nor was his logic abstruse or recondite. His mental processes were not tortuous nor were his emotional reactions too involved. More often wise than brilliant, he was a man of primitive rugged strength. Human enough to be vain, he could never be flattered or cajoled out of the orbit of his moral convictions.

No Jew of Ussishkin's generation was better integrated as a human being, as a Jew and as a Zionist. In the Russia of his early youth, the liberal currents of the day did not leave him untouched. Yet, they did not wash away his Jewish roots as liberal currents sometimes do. Culturally, Ussishkin was rooted in Biblical and Rabbinic tradition, yet Russian and European culture were also an integral part of his endowment. Spiritually, he was rooted in the Faith of his fathers, yet none of his Jewish contemporaries was more responsive to the practical need of the hour, or appreciated more keenly the futility of faith unaccompanied by deeds. His Zionism stemmed from Jewish tradition and came to flower under the nourishing rays of Pinsker, Lilienblum and Ahad Ha'am, yet he made his own unique contributions to the Zionist program.

Ussishkin, being well integrated himself, was an integrating force among his Zionist contemporaries and the basic ideas which starred their Zionist horizon. Recognizing the pre-eminence of the whole over its parts, he sought to keep together the segments which now and then threatened to fall apart. In this sense he was the General Zionist "par excellence." Hashomer Hatzair on the left and Mizrachi on the right, the Mapai* party and the Revisionists at the opposite poles, they all felt, claimed and found a share in him. To the extent that one man can honestly and genuinely keep all wings under his wing, he was the man. No other leader in the Yishuv was esteemed and trusted so much by so many.

Ussishkin was the General Zionist also in a functional sense. Everything worthwhile in the life of the Yishuv was his concern. No other man touched its life at so many points and nurtured it with such fructifying care. Land redemption, immigration and colonization, the organization of the Yishuv into a democratically functioning unity, its politics, its self-defense and the education of its youth, all came within the province of his interest and concern and in diverse degrees fell within the scope of his official jurisdiction.

That the crowning labor of his life should have been *Geulath Ha'aretz* was utterly in key with the contour of his career. *Emet Me-Eretz Titzmah,* truth springs from the soil. Nature is without guile. Mother Earth holds together and feeds the roots of field and forest, as well as of the good society. Land, the most fundamental of life's commodities is the first object of human greed. Therefore the just social use and possession of land is the prime criterion of a just social order. The symbol of the Jewish tragedy is landlessness. The rehabilitation of the Jewish

---

*Mapai—The Hebrew name for the Palestine Labor Party.

people must begin, therefore, with its return to the soil. The *Aleph* of Zionism is inevitably *Eretz,* land in Eretz Israel. *Geulath Ha'aretz* was, most naturally, the *Aleph* in the index of Ussishkin's ideals and responsibilities.

Perhaps the most impressive element of Ussishkin's life was his consistency. That quality gave the aspect of integrated unity to his career. It was a consistency, to all evidence, which sprang from the roots of his being. Though events colored the terms, they did not change the direction of his thought and of his will. Those who called it *Akshanuth,* obstinacy, might have perceived it, on second thought, as a true phase of integrity.

Professor Klausner's biography of Ussishkin sheds illuminating light upon all the aspects of his personality. With simple artistry the biographer traces the consistency of the career, showing how his mature commitments and labors had their origins in his youth. Ussishkin himself derived considerable satisfaction from parallels of his student days with his manly life. The famous "Ussishkin map" of later years, a standing challenge to Jewish land redemption, had its antecedent in the map of Palestine which was hung on his wall in his student days. His great service to the Hebrew University and the educational system in the Yishuv was prototyped by a student society for cultural activity at the Technical High School in Moscow where the twenty-year-old student delivered his first lecture on the "Maccabean Revolt." At the same time he was engaged in the practical work of fund raising, distributing and collecting boxes for the settlement of the Land of Israel, long before it became a standard Keren Kayemeth technique. Already he was a conciliatory influence in the conflicts between the religious and the secular Zionists. Already he advocated the creation of a farmer class in Palestine, asserted that Jerusalem must be the heart of Jewish Palestine and the place of its national library, and exhorted Jewish young men to consecrate years of their lives to the settlement of Eretz Israel.

Thus the architectonic unity of Ussishkin's life becomes overwhelmingly clear in Professor Klausner's outline. Klausner, the biographer, is not always able to dissociate himself from Klausner, the colleague of Ussishkin. But there is no rule that biography must be objective. There is an advantage in writing chronicles from the fresh mainsprings of personal association rather than from dusty archives. Klausner's volume breathes and pulsates.

The difficulty encountered by a biographer where the subject is but a few months dead, is that of perspective. None of us today can foretell with certainly how the constituent parts of Ussishkin's life will emerge in the perspective of the years.

It is reward enough to those who knew Ussishkin, to see set down in the printed page an authentic word image of the best integrated Jew of our time, whose Jewishness was whole, whose commanding presence at Zionist Congresses was itself an outstanding feature of the convocation, whose moral sturdiness was as much respected by his foes as admired by his friends, and who will probably go down in the history of the Zionist movement, together with Chaim Weizmann, as next only to Theodor Herzl.

To those who never beheld the man, this story will illustrate the Ussishkin legend which is already a part of the *Otzar Israel,* the "Jewish National Fund" embracing the saga of Israel's national heroes.

A sequel volume will appear shortly, to consist of Ussishkin's addresses without which his biography would not be complete.

The publication of this book, timed to coincide with the first anniversary of Menahem Ussishkin's death, adumbrates one episode of the *Netzah Israel*—the eternity of Israel, and the life of one of its sons who will remain immortal in the soil and in the soul of that people.

Dr. Israel Goldstein

Introduction

IT IS NO EASY TASK TO WRITE A BOOK ABOUT THE FRIEND of one's youth, the man one knew intimately for many a decade. It is hardest of all to write about him when his death took place less than a year ago and one cannot yet believe that the great man, the great fighter, the great friend, is really gone.

And how can one treat such a rich and active life adequately in a book written so soon after the passing of the man? Necessarily, this volume treats only of the high points of Ussishkin's sixty years of public life and must omit a multitude of details, many of them interesting and important. Nor has it been possible to do more than summarize Menahem Ussishkin's most significant speeches and articles. Yet it may be that, precisely because of these limitations, the most memorable aspects of Ussishkin's activity will be more clearly emphasized.

Let this little book, then, be as a tribute laid in sorrow upon the fresh grave of the great man and the never-to-be-forgotten friend.

J. K.

I

Childhood and Youth

MENAHEM (MENDEL) SON OF REB MOSES ZVI Ussishkin was born on Rosh Hodesh Ellul 5623 (August 14, 1863) at Dubrovna village in the Mohilev District of White Russia. His father was a Lithuanian *Habad* Hassid,* good-hearted, God-fearing and blessed with a straightforward level-headedness. His mother, Reiza of the Berlin family, was a shrewd woman of considerable will-power and a sharp brain, hale both in body and mind, who lived to a good old age, retaining until the last a keen understanding of the new developments around her, and losing none of her own dominant will. It is said that every great man has an exceptional mother and is a mixture of the antithetical qualities of both his parents. Ussishkin is unquestionably an example of such a combination, and had a mother of unusual character.

Until the age of eight Ussishkin lived with his parents at Dubrovna, a community famous at one time for the weaving of prayer-shawls which it supplied to all the Jewish congregations in Russia. He was the only son of his

---

*The *Habad* Hassidim were found chiefly in and round Lithuania, and their religious approach was less emotional and more philosophical and scholarly than that of other Hassidic groups—in the early days of Hassidism at least.

father and mother; of his sisters four died during childhood, leaving one who died when she was a young woman. It was natural in such circumstances that the parents should tend to pamper their only son, and signs of this were to persist during his whole life. He was a good-looking boy, and this also made him popular. It was partly his easy childhood which led to the great demands he made on life, and to his obstinate and determined insistence on his own viewpoint; but it also produced his strength of will, his love of life and his capacity for work.

In 1867, when he was four years old, his parents sent him to the *Heder* (private Hebrew class), as was the custom in those days. There he remained from morning to night until 1871, learning steadily. This was the particular care of his grandfather who would not permit any of the child's time to run to waste. During those four years the little boy learned the greater part of the Bible and two tractates of the Talmud.

In 1871 his parents moved from Dubrovna to Moscow. Reb Moshe Zvi Ussishkin was a wealthy merchant and was therefore able to receive permission to reside in Moscow, though this was denied to the overwhelming majority of Jews. Here Menahem continued his Hebrew studies, practically without any change, for five whole years from 1871 to 1876. Reb Haim Berlin, the Rabbi of Moscow and son of the famous Naphtali Zvi Yehuda Berlin, head of the Volozhin Yeshivah which was renowned in East European Jewry, had engaged a learned scholar to teach his only son and allowed the young Menahem, related to the Berlins through his mother, to participate in these studies. In this way the boy perfected his knowl-

MENAHEM USSISHKIN'S FATHER: MOSHE ZVI; HIS MOTHER: REIZA

USSISHKIN AND HIS FAMILY IN 1935

Childhood and Youth

edge of Bible and Talmud, studying nothing else until his Bar Mitzva at the age of thirteen. The Bar Mitzva of Ussishkin was the occasion of great family celebrations, and in honor of the event his parents presented a scroll of the Torah to the Synagogue. When Ussishkin came to Jerusalem he brought the scroll of the Torah with him and it is now kept in the Jeshurun Synagogue at Rehavia.

After the Bar Mitzva celebration in 1876, Menahem's life entered on a new phase. His father decided to send him to the Technical School of Moscow. After all, Ussishkin's father was a wealthy merchant; and Moscow was not Dubrovna. It was clearly impossible to let the son of a Moscow Jewish merchant do without a general European education. In addition, like many pious Jews who were not extremists, Reb Moshe Zvi cherished the belief that it was possible to combine complete orthodoxy with a wide range of general culture. The only obstacles in the way of entry to the school were the observance of Sabbaths and festivals; for as the school was not one for Jews excusively, it was open on those days. Reb Moshe Zvi Ussishkin thereupon applied to the Russian Minister of Education for his son to be exempted from the requirement of attending school and examinations at such times; and his application was favorably received, so that young Menahem's education did not conflict with his religious upbringing. In the afternoons he continued his Jewish studies after his return from school. The young student was particularly happy as a result of this combination of Jewish and general studies, and did not feel that there was the slightest breach between his faith and his culture.

In 1878, two years later, when Menahem was fifteen

years old, his father engaged an instructor for him in Modern Hebrew Literature and Grammar. This teacher was one of the leading *Maskilim** of the period, Benjamin Grodzinsky of Slutsk, and he exerted a considerable influence upon his pupil. As reading matter he gave the boy the works of Mapu, Smolenskin and Kalman Schulman, and introduced him to *Hashahar* and *Hamelitz*, the leading Hebrew periodicals of the day. These were the first unconscious seeds of Zionism and Jewish nationalism to be sown in the heart of the youngster. Thanks to them it came about that despite young Menahem's idealistic character and the interest in public affairs which he evinced from his earliest youth, he was not swept away by the general trend of the time. He did not join the Russian revolutionary movement which was then so widespread among the pupils of all the secondary schools in Russia. Religious orthodoxy on the one hand, and the unconsciously but deeply nationalist Hebrew literature of the period on the other, shielded him from following this general Russian movement. In addition, the words of Mapu and Schulman had already aroused within him a singular even if vague emotional feeling with regard to the Land of Israel. When, for instance, the Hebrew press published an advertisement of the first Hebrew map of Palestine, the young Ussishkin hastened to purchase it and hung it on the wall of his room. It almost seemed as though he foresaw that the time would come when he would be engaged primarily on the map of the Land of

---

* The *Maskilim* were the participants in the *Haskala* or Enlightenment movement which was one of the leading internal Jewish factors in the secularization of Central and East European Jewry during the nineteenth century.

Israel, in order to know every stretch of land which could be purchased for the Jewish people. . . .

On the last day of Passover 5641 (April, 1881) a series of pogroms commenced in Southern Russia and continued with brief interruptions for two years. It is hard now to recall the effect of these unforeseen calamities on world Jewry in general and the Jews of Russia in particular. They came like a bolt from the blue to the Jewish *Maskilim* and intellectuals who had relied on enlightened Europe and believed that "persecution of the Jews was possible only in backward Asia." They did not even have the partial comfort that the Russian masses had no support in these excesses. Not only did the Russian police and army stand by while Jews were beaten and robbed for no other reason than that they were Jews, but even the Russian intellectuals saw no reason to make any strong protest. Russian socialists went so far as to declare brazenly that it was a good thing for the masses to become accustomed to attacking the Jews, since this would train them to revolt against Russian autocracy and the entire capitalist system. Russian journals to which cultured writers contributed, justified the anti-Jewish excesses by declaring that the Jews were foreigners in Russia and were injurious to the "dominant race"; and that an educated Jew, whether writer, physician or lawyer, was more dangerous to the Russians as a gifted competitor than the ordinary religious Jew. . . .

Russian Jewry was shaken to its very roots. A communal fast was proclaimed in virtually every Jewish community in Russia. The synagogues were thronged not merely by religious Jews but equally by Jewish students of the secondary schools and the universities. Ussishkin and his friend, Yehiel Tchlenov, attended the services, and the impression made on them was tremendous; Ussishkin was eighteen years old at the time.

A short while afterwards he and Tchlenov learned that a new national movement had sprung into being among the students with the watchword: "O House of Jacob, come and let us go!"* Let us forsake Europe and its culture, which has proved so useless to the Jewish people in their hour of need when violence was done them in the full light of the sun. Let us forsake Europe where we are strangers, and let us return to Asia whence we came and where we saw the vision of peace and international fraternity, the vision of the Jewish prophets; where it will be impossible to taunt us any longer with being strangers and foreigners. The Bible stands as witness that the land is ours and that it is the land of our fathers; and there we shall not be charged with living as petty merchants and hawkers and innkeepers (a common Jewish calling in Eastern Europe) at the expense of others. Yonder we shall till the soil of our forefathers and eat the daily bread produced by our own toil, like all the nations who dwell upon earth.

These ideas won over the two young friends, Ussishkin and Tchlenov. When they heard that there was to be a meeting of nationalist students (who were referred to at the time as "Jewish patriots") in Moscow, they begged and entreated to be allowed to participate. However, they were not university students but high school pupils; hence

---

*BILU (the initials of the words in the Biblical phrase "Beth Jacob Lechu Venelcha," found in Isaiah, Chapter II).

they could not be granted the rights and privileges of students. Thereupon they proposed that they should be allowed to distribute the invitations to the meeting. (It was not advisable to send them by post as the meeting was naturally being held without the permission of the authorities.) In return for this they were permitted to be present at the meeting, which was held on January 1, 1882, and at which a fierce debate promptly began.

The subject of the debate was: which destination? Since it was clear that there was no hope for Russian Jewry within Russia, the question obviously arose as to the country to which they should emigrate. Should it be America or the Land of Israel? The students split into two groups. One was opposed to Asia. Enlightened Europe, they argued, had to be left because its enlightenment could not be relied upon, but in that case it would certainly be foolish to leave it for "savage Asia." America was the land of freedom, where riots were impossible (as the Hebrew poet, J. L. Gordon, had proclaimed in one of his poems).

The other group, however, stood firm in their view that the only place where the Jewish people could return to life with its Torah and its own tongue was the land in which the people of Israel had come into being, where their kings and prophets had arisen. There, and only there, would the Jewish people not remain alien in the eyes of the dominant nationality. In their hearts Ussishkin and Tchlenov agreed with the latter group, but since they were merely guests at this meeting of students, they could not find any means of expressing their opinions. So they resolved to establish their own "Society of Immigrants to the Land of Israel," for the purpose of leaving Russian at once and proceeding to the Land of Israel in order to till its soil. Ussishkin always reckoned his term of service in the Jewish national movement as commencing on the great day when he and his friends founded this society for immigration to the Land of Israel, without knowing that the Bilu already existed as an organized movement and something more than a watchword.

A fortnight later they were joined by another high school boy, Hissin, who proposed as member a girl named Fania Pariser, later to be Mrs. Hissin. Little by little the society grew till it had twenty-five members, including three girls. Hissin raised the question: Why must it be the Land of Israel and nowhere else? And only after prolonged debates did he agree that the most suitable country for the establishment of the Jewish State was the Land of Israel.

In the intermediary days of Passover 5642 (1882) the twenty-five members of the society met for the inaugural meeting at which a very grave question came under discussion; namely, the constitution of the Jewish State in the Land of Israel. Hissin wished for a republic with a president to be elected every seventh year in the year of *Shemita* (the Biblical Sabbatical year). Tchlenov wished for a constitutional monarchy, and Ussishkin desired an autocracy like the House of David in the days of the Bible. The debates continued for whole nights on end, and finally Hissen triumphed. It stands to reason; young Jews in Russia, if they were studying at the secondary schools, mostly retained their left-wing tendencies even after they became Zionists. By reason of his traditionalism

Ussishkin was an exception, and in addition was already developing his own specific attitude.

After they had resolved on the constitution, they set out to collect funds. To this end Ussishkin pawned the gold watch which he had received as a Bar Mitzva gift. They collected a total of 475 roubles and naively felt certain that this money would be sufficient to bring all twenty-five of them to the Land of Israel, the haven of their desire. Meanwhile they learned that in Kharkov a society of young people who were prepared to go up to the Land of Israel had already been established and had actually taken the name Bilu. It was only natural for the Moscow Society to propose that the two groups should make the journei to the Land of Israel together. The Biluites responded that they would be prepared to accept the young Muscovites after they had met them; and they sent a special delegate to Moscow for the purpose.

The Kharkov delegate arrived and proposed that the Moscow Society should become a branch of the Kharkov Bilu. He also explained that 475 roubles would not be sufficient to transport twenty-five people, and was enough only for seven. It was therefore necessary to elect seven of the twenty-five for the purpose. Following a long speech by Hissin, he was elected together with Fania Pariser, Drubin who was a bookkeeper, Tzalalichin who was a blacksmith, and another three who left Palestine after they had been there a single month. Ussishkin and Tchlenov were not elected. They were regarded as children of plutocrats, and therefore spoilt in their upbringing and not suited for tilling the soil. Ussishkin wept when he was not elected. It was certainly the first, and perhaps the only, time in his life that he did so.

What would have happened if he had been elected? Is it possible even to guess how his life and activities would have shaped themselves in the course of decades, and how the whole Zionist movement would have developed under such circumstances?

II

Work in the Movement Begins

THOUGH USSISHKIN WAS NOT ELECTED ONE OF THE Biluites who were to leave for the Land of Israel, the new national movement had won his heart and he began to take an active part in it. In those days an active part meant the organizing of Hovevei Zion societies and the collection of funds for the settlement of the Land of Israel. The young Ussishkin engaged in both.

In Moscow as in most other large cities of Russia, a society of bourgeois "Hovevei Zion" was established, to which belonged wealthy Jewish merchants who were versed in Jewish learning and were also *Maskilim,* intellectuals of the "enlightened" type. They were more or less orthodox but all conservative. Ussishkin participated in this society, attending its meetings and helping to raise money for the establishment of settlements in Palestine.

Yet he did not rest satisfied with that. He was a young intellectual, and, after all, his place was not among well-established folk whose chief interest was fund-raising. He wished to work among youngsters, and to find some sort of activity that was both practical and cultural.

In the summer of 1883 he completed his course at the "Real" school and in the autumn of the same year entered the Technical High School of Moscow. And thereupon he established a student society for cultural activities. The members of the society included Jacob Maze and Yehiel Levontin, who afterwards gained considerable reputations, the former as Rabbi of Moscow and the latter as a Hebrew writer under the nom de plume of *Hushai Ha-archi*. It was in this society that Ussishkin delivered his first lecture. The theme he chose is interesting for he spoke on "The Maccabean Revolt." The nineteen-year-old youth already felt that there was something rebellious and revolutionary in the youthful and quiet movement known as "Hibbat Zion," or Hovevei Zion, as its supporters were called.

In August 1884 the "Bnei Zion" or Sons of Zion Society was founded in Moscow with the purpose of organizing the academic Jewish youth for cultural and educational work in a national and Zionist spirit (or "Palestinian" spirit, as it was then called). To begin with, only seven students belonged to this society. They included Ussishkin, Tchlenov, Yehiel Levontin, A. L. Mintz, Shlomo Mintz, etc. It was to exert a vast influence on the development of Hibbat Zion and later on Zionism, and many important Zionist leaders and workers came from its ranks. About sixty members, male and female, participated in the inaugural meeting. The committee elected on this occasion included Tchlenov as chairman, Levontin as secretary and Ussishkin as librarian of what was the first Hebrew library in Moscow. Ussishkin's fondness for literature alongside his devotion to practical work was already apparent.

By the time that Ussishkin was a young student of

Work in the Movement Begins

twenty-one, it had become obvious to him that without real concrete activities the new movement would remain the same disembodied wraith as the Messianic hopes of our forefathers, which were never realized. Yet the meager results of the efforts of the Hovevei Zion might well have made him and others dispirited and brought the entire movement to nothing. No sooner had the wave of immigration to Palestine commenced on a more or less appreciable scale than Turkey closed the doors to immigrants. Further, the Russian government regarded with disfavor every movement of any kind in the country, for the tyrannical autocracy of Czar Alexander III was then in full sway.

Such was the external situation. Within the Jewish community the closing of Palestine to immigration led to a deep feeling of futility, and the opponents of Hibbat Zion became numerous, including even the talented writers Sokolow and Frischmann.* If the earliest Hovevei Zion were to suspend their small-scale but real activities of maintaining the few settlements already established in the country, there was a very considerable danger that the entire movement might dwindle to nothing. For this reason Ussishkin engaged in cultural activities such as the purchase of Hebrew books, canvassing for subscriptions to the Hebrew press and the study of Jewish history; he also

---

*Nahum Sokolow changed his views later, and ultimately became President of the Zionist Organization. A man of astounding range of knowledge and culture, he was the dean of Jewish journalists and publicists. His "History of Zionism" and "The Philosophy of Hibbat Zion" have been translated into English. David Frischmann was a leading Hebrew and Yiddish publicist, literary critic and translator, whose views carried vast weight in their day.

organized societies and conducted propaganda among all sections of the Jewish community, at first in Moscow alone but later throughout Russia. Furthermore, he engaged in fund-raising, in the distribution to Jewish homes, and the clearance, of collection-boxes for the settlement of the Land of Israel. The success of such "minor activities" gave fresh confidence to the weary and revived fading hopes. In 1885 Ussishkin was elected secretary of all the Hovevei Zion societies in Moscow, and his work began to be both many-sided and exceedingly productive.

He was the first person to appreciate the tremendous value of written and spoken propaganda. Under his influence and that of Tchlenov the Moscow societies supported the publication of works imbued with the national and Zionist spirit, such as Lilienblum's Russian volume, "The Revival of Israel in the Fatherland," and the Russian miscellany, "Palestine." The societies endeavored to enlarge the number of subscribers to *Hamelitz* which had become the Hebrew organ of the Hovevei Zion, and offered a prize for the best Hebrew national poem. But Ussishkin also called for "Zionist orators," a new development of the ancient *Maggidim* or homilists who spoke in the synagogue, in order to spread the Zionist idea among the Jewish masses. The tremendous value of the work of men of this type such as Masliansky, Yevzerov and others was generally recognized. Ussishkin corresponded with the leaders of the movement and with everyone to whom the movement and the Yishuv were of interest. From 1887 onwards he began to publish letters in *Hamelitz* on matters appertaining to the movement and problems of the Yishuv; later he began to write essays of his own touching on

Hibbat Zion. Here he set out to reconcile those who had become estranged from the movement, to make the Hovevei Zion moderate and patient, to persuade them to unite and gather their strength. For him Hibbat Zion was not only a great vision but also a vast and outstanding practical undertaking. He knew that the activity connected with it must lead to national unity, and national unity in turn would produce revival and liberation.

For this reason, despite the fact that he was still a student and a member of a student society, he did something which to all appearances was hardly to be expected of an enlightened student like him. Following in his father's footsteps he was a Habad Hassid, and therefore, almost at the end of 1886, he turned to the Rabbi of Kapust, the leader of all Habad Hassidim, and asked for an interview in order to discuss the settlement of Palestine. The rabbi received him very graciously, and for an hour and a half the young student explained the material and spiritual foundations and aspirations of the Hibbat Zion movement. The rabbi was enchanted by this student who combined fear of the Lord with Western culture, and permitted himself to say that he approved of Hibbat Zion which "tends to unite all hearts" and would therefore advise anybody prepared to ask his counsel, "to do as much for the Hovevei Zion as he could." Ussishkin promptly published in *Hamelitz* the words of the rabbi, which were sacred counsel to all Habad Hassidim; and the young student immediately became known in interested circles as one of the most active members of the Hovevei Zion.

He was appointed joint secretary with Lilienblum to the

Druskenik Conference, which met on June 16, 1887. He came to this Conference as Moscow delegate and had a double duty to perform. The Hovevei Zion Organization had been established at the Kattowitz Conference in 1884, and had combined two currents: the orthodox and the secular. The differences between these two came to a head at the Druskenik Conference. Rabbi Samuel Mohilever led the orthodox and was dissatisfied because the movement was headed by persons who were free-thinkers and who supported the rights of the Bilu student settlers at Gedera more than those of the orthodox farmers of Petah Tikva. The free-thinkers and secularists were headed by Pinkser and Lilienblum, the theoretical and practical initiators of the Hibbat Zion movement. Rabbi Mohilever demanded the resignation of Lilienblum, whose rationlist and anti-orthodox works, "Sins of Youth" and "Ways of the Talmud" had not yet been forgotten or forgiven. Pinsker, who found Lilienblum to be his right hand in all that concerned the movement outside Palestine and within the youthful Yishuv of that country, objected vehemently to his resignation; and all the younger men and intellectuals stood behind him. However, Rabbi Mohilever was supported by the famous head of the Volozhin Yeshiva, Rabbi N. Z. J. Berlin and all the remaining Hovevei Zion rabbis, and had a considerable party at Druskenik. If these two opposing groups had come into conflict at the Conference, and if no means of mediating between them had been found, the entire Hibbat Zion movement might have reached a state of explosion the outcome of which would have been difficult to foresee. The pious student Ussishkin endeavored to find some means of reconciling Rabbi Mohilever and his party on the one hand and Pinsker, Lilienblum and their supporters on the other. He was equally acceptable to both sides, being on the one hand an engineering student and hence an intellectual, and on the other an observer of Jewish laws and commandments like the most orthodox. To some degree he saved the situation by bringing the extreme opponents to an agreement, so that peace was established regarding the affairs of the Yishuv in Palestine.

Such was Ussishkin's first important activity at the Druskenik Conference.

His second was the submission to the Conference of the proposals of the Moscow Hovevei Zion, in which his own approach could be clearly felt.

These proposals were briefly as follows:

The Hovevei Zion Organization should be entrusted to a committee of five, all resident in the same city and dealing with administration, propaganda, collection of funds and settlement. Funds collected should be expended not only in support of the older settlers but also for the purchase of new areas of land and the establishment of fresh settlements. When redeeming land, quality and area should not be regarded as of prime importance. Everything that could be purchased should be purchased, even though it might be impossible to settle people thereon immediately. Persons entirely without means should not be settled, but priority should be given to those with resources of their own who would require only a little aid. This would make it possible to settle larger numbers of Jews on the land while keeping the allocation of support at a low level; for it would be impossible to redeem Zion by charity alone, and more than donations were required for the revival of the land and the people.

As regards propaganda, it ought to aim at "spreading the idea of settling the country and reviving the nation," and must set out "to increase the desire of the people to ascend to the land of their fathers and settle there." For this end it was not only necessary to issue books and pamphlets and to hold frequent speeches and lectures on the idea of settlement in the Land of Israel and the national revival there; it was also necessary to disseminate definite information on the settlement of the country, its climate, soil, commerce and conditions of life.

Ussishkin spoke in support of these proposals at the Druskenik Conference. And though they were not passed officially, because the internal disputes took up most of the time, his words nevertheless made an impression and in the course of time had their effect on the Hibbat Zion movement.

III

The First Journey to the Land of Israel

IN 1889, AT TWENTY-SIX, USSISHKIN GRADUATED FROM the Moscow Technical High School with the degree of Technological Engineer. At about the same time, he published two essays in *Hamelitz*, one entitled, "Regarding the Belief That 'The Study of the Torah Is More Than All Else,'" and the second entitled, "Why Weaken the Hands of the People?"

The first essay dealt with the proposal of Prof. Hermann Schapira to establish a university in Jerusalem, and that of Eliezer Ben Yehuda to found a rabbinical seminary there. It was the opinion of Ussishkin that nobody but a visionary could at that time think of a university in Palestine. First and foremost, we aspired to the creation in Palestine of a farmer class whose sons would not be "huge heads on chicken feet" but ordinary people tilling the soil. Secondly, would young Jews and Jewish professors, the overwhelming majority of whom were assimilationists, leave the universities of Europe in order to study and teach in the Land of Israel? Thirdly, where would the money be found for a university when we did not even have sufficient money to support Petah Tikva, Gedera and Yessod Hamaaleh, the three settlements which Baron de Rothschild had not yet taken charge of at that time? As regards the rabbinical seminary, not a single Jewish community in

Western Europe would accept a rabbi from Palestine, while the Russian communities were almost all orthodox and the orthodox Jews in Palestine itself would rise up with all their might against such an institution. Only one thing was possible: to unite the *yeshivoth* (talmudical colleges) which already existed in Palestine, and convert them into one fine central institution. This would require a relatively small expenditure and would not lead to the destruction of anything already in existence.

The second essay was "An Open Letter to Zalman David Levontin," the Hovev Zion who had founded Rishon le-Zion, even before the coming of the Bilu. Levontin had published articles in the press at that time proposing that not only agriculture but also industry should be engaged in, since that was the only way whereby considerable results could be achieved; for the pennies collected as donations by the Hovevei Zion were few and meager. Ussishkin turned on him with a question that was a rebuke. "Why do you weaken the hands of the people?" For the present, it is impossible even to seek people prepared to invest large sums in Palestine industry, and the pennies which our brethren donate on behalf of the Yishuv are the only real standard of measurement of the love of Zion and the conscious readiness to do things on behalf of the new Yishuv which, though of small beginnings, will finally grow great. For "any activity, even the least and smallest, may ultimately lead to large-scale activities, and therefore it is much better than sitting with arms folded until the time comes for large-scale activities; for what is in existence is infinitely greater than that which is not in existence, as the pound is more than the penny."

We see here before us the whole attitude of Ussishkin as he was to maintain it throughout his life, until his very last day.

In Spring 1889, the Bnei Moshe Society commenced activities with Ahad Ha'am at its head and with Lilienblum as one of its original members. Both of them wrote a joint letter to Ussishkin requesting him to join. To begin with, Ussishkin refused because the regulations of the Society did not, to his mind, sufficiently stress the practical, settlement activities of Hibbat Zion. But Joshua Barzillai (Eisenstadt) came and persuaded Ussishkin with his fiery enthusiasm, and Ussishkin not only became a member of the Bnei Moshe but also proposed a constitution for the Society which, however, was not accepted by Ahad Ha'am and his comrades. Thenceforward Ussishkin became an active member and, without giving up his preference for practical work in Palestine, devoted himself heart and soul to cultural national activity in the Diaspora along the lines of Ahad Ha'am.

As one of the Bnei Moshe and its Moscow representative, he participated in the inaugural meeting of the "Committee for the Support of Jewish Tillers of the Soil and Artisans in Syria and Palestine" or, more briefly, the Hovevei Zion Committee in Odessa. The meeting was held in Spring 1890, at Odessa, and was preceded by important unofficial sessions at which Ussishkin stood out as one of the chief speakers regarding Yishuv affairs, and one of the chief workers on behalf of the movement as a whole. At the Bnei Moshe Conference which was held at the same time in Odessa, Dr. Chazanowitz proposed the establishment in Palestine of a national library. Most of the members were in favor of establishing it at Jaffa, which was then the center of the Jewish settlements, but Ussishkin devoted all his eloquence to claiming Jerusalem as the place for the foundation of the National Library, because Jerusalem is the heart of the nation and the center of its spirit and culture. Ussishkin's proposal was passed unanimously.

Here, too, we see Ussishkin in his early youth, supporting an idea with which he was imbued throughout his life. There is no true center for Israel except Jerusalem. And this was at the very time when Lilienblum, for example was prepared to renounce Jerusalem in his book, "The Revival of Israel in the Fatherland," in order not to enter into conflict with the Christians to whom Jerusalem was equally holy.

Early in 1891, Ussishkin married Esther Palai of Ekaterinoslav, with whom he lived happily for fifty years. For his honeymoon, he chose to take his bride to Palestine. This was something very unusual in those days, and led the Hebrew writer, A. L. Levinsky, to write his remarkable "Journey to Palestine in the Year 2040." Ussishkin spent seven weeks in the country and passed through the length and breadth thereof, which was by no means an easy feat under the conditions of the time when there were no railways and scarcely as much as a road. During his journey, he kept a diary in Russian which he published in 1894. A Hebrew translation of this diary, entitled "Journey to the Land of Israel," was published in "Sefer Ussishkin."

All the qualities which characterized his Zionist viewpoint and activities on behalf of the Yishuv are to be found in this first brochure of the young Ussishkin. Every political,

The First Journey to the Land of Israel

economic and cultural phenomenon which he saw in town and country in Palestine he submitted to the test of his own clear and keen observation, and judged it from the viewpoint of its future results. For this reason, together with all the realism of his examination and the precision and brevity of his style, this pamphlet is full of vision, scope and Zionist romanticism of the highest kind, that romanticism which does not disregard realities but adds something to them by strengthening faith in ultimate possibilities, and makes us conscious that little things are only a stage on the way to great things. . . .

Thus he writes, for example, about his first visit to the Wailing Wall:

> There was a crowd of worshippers in front of it. All of them were reciting the afternoon prayers. But I did not pray. What I saw with my mind's eye was the life which went on here two thousand years ago, and I described to myself what used to happen then at this place and at this season, the Eve of Passover. Then, too, Jews flocked hither from the ends of the earth. Yonder on Mount Moriah, where the Moslem Mosque now stands, our Temple then rose. This wall was already in existence, but instead of being a remnant of the past was part of a living whole. Then, as well, a vast multitude was to be found here, but instead of weeping at their prayers, they rejoiced and praised their God. . . . No. I shall leave these weepers and return another time when nobody stands by; and then these grey stones will speak to me in another tongue.

He was very orthodox in those days, but nevertheless did not pray beside the Wall when his unorthodox friends did so. And he, the man most engaged in public life, the public speaker, who was always working to influence the masses, sought isolation at the moment when first he visited the sacred vestige of the past; he wished to be alone with the silent stones and his own sad thoughts. And he behaved thus throughout his life. From time to time, he would visit the Wall alone and commune with it. When I came to Jerusalem in 1920, for the purpose of settling here, my first visit was to Ussishkin. It was a cold and wet evening during the Jerusalem winter. But we left the gathering of writers and communal workers who had come to Ussishkin's home to converse with the guest, and at ten in the evening, in the cold and the dark, went down to the Wall. There we sat, Ussishkin, another man and myself, for about half an hour in the small open space in front of the Wall, each deep in his thoughts; not one of us opening his mouth or saying a word to the other. . . . And in the same dumb silence we rose and returned through the dark night along the paths and through the dead, narrow streets of the Jerusalem of those days to Ussishkin's home. . . .

That was the strongest impression of the Wall which we both experienced. . . . I always remember that visit, and Ussishkin also told me that he could not forget it. The darkness, the silence and the loneliness—how greatly they suit the orphanhood of the holy Wall.

Before Ussishkin left Jerusalem on his first visit, he came to take his leave of the Wall and he wrote: "I was lucky. I found nobody beside the Wall. And I stood there alone, together with my thoughts and impressions.

It is a popular belief that anybody who takes a chip of stone from the Wall will know no rest in any place or at any time until he comes back and returns the chip to its place. But it seems to me that anybody who has stood beside the Wall and has seen it once in his life will know no rest in his soul until he returns here again."

And sure enough, Ussishkin returned here a third and a fourth time, and afterwards on countless occasions. . . .

There is another part of his diary which particularly deserves to be quoted here.

He had gone with several companions to the Valley of Jehoshophat and had reached the Pillar of Absalom. He saw the spot from which the Romans besieged Jerusalem at the time of the destruction of the Temple. And once again he wrote:

> Here I moved some distance away from the others, and sank into my thoughts. Before my eyes, passed the figures of our ancient heroes, who gave their lives to protect our Temple. In the eyes of the spirit I saw passing before me those great men, Simeon bar Giora and Yohannan of Gush Hulav, who held that it was better to lose everything than to continue a miserable existence in subjection to Rome. Where are you, where are you, oh heroes? You have perished, and with you has perished our heroic spirit. We have become shrewd and practical. Now we say, *Ubi bene ibi patria* (where things are good, there is the Fatherland); we shall return to your land only when conditions are satisfactory there for us. Oh for shame!

Ussishkin, one of the leading practical men of our movement, could rise above the practical men of the familiar shrewd type and could esteem those heroes and fighting statesmen who did not believe in the principle, "It is better to be a living dog than a dead lion.'" He, on the contrary, believed that "life is not the most precious thing in life"—the thought of all those who today are fighting against tyranny and aggression, and who are prepared to risk everything for the sake of freedom.

But Ussishkin saw in the Land of Israel not only the greatness and pride of the past. He also saw the pettiness and contemptibility of the present, the personal considerations and the speculators who were chaffering with the great ideals of the nation.

Nevertheless, when Ahad Ha'am published his essay, "Truth from the Land of Israel" in *Hamelitz*, in the summer of 1891, Ussishkin countered with another essay, entitled "Without Excessive Pessimism," in which he showed that the situation was not quite so black as Ahad Ha'am described it. Ussishkin declared that he had not expected to see much that was satisfactory when he went to Palestine; therefore, whatever he found to be good made him rejoice and gave him reason to hope that this difficult beginning would find a satisfactory continuation and glorious ending. Hence Ussishkin's optimism was the outcome of his realistic view of the situation in Palestine. It was far more justified than was the pessimism of Ahad Ha'am, who had without justification expected great things at the commencement of activities and was, therefore, so disappointed that he could not appraise the good which was unquestionably already to be found in the country.

IV

The Beginnings of Political Zionism

From Palestine, Ussishkin returned not to Moscow, but to Ekaterinoslav, where his father-in-law resided. He stayed there for fifteen years, from 1891 until 1906.

The Hovevei Zion Committee, established in Odessa in 1890, had sent to Jaffa the Engineer Zeev Tiomkin, one of the leading idealists and orators among the Hovevei Zion, in order that he might head the Palestine Executive of the movement. The stormy days of the movement now began. Dozens of societies were established and sent their representatives to purchase land in Palestine, upon which extensive speculation broke out and the price of land commenced to rise. Turkey, startled at the large number of immigrants, closed Palestine to Jews, and a considerable crisis at once ensued in the entire settlement movement.

Large sums which had been paid in advance to Arab landowners were lost, because the Jewish purchasers decided to withdraw from their undertakings after the closing of the gates, and in view of the bad reports which arrived. Naturally, this influenced the state of mind throughout the Hibbat Zion movement. The rise was followed by a fall. Practical work declined. Further, the high hopes of vast sums to be received by the Hovevei Zion were also disappointed. The Jews of the entire

Russian Empire, including Poland, Lithuania, etc., amounted to some ten million; yet they did not provide more than 30,000-40,000 rubles for Palestine purposes, which amounted to some £3,000-£4,000 or $15,000-$20,000 at the time. Many of the Hovevei Zion were disappointed and withdrew from the movement, but the best of them continued to collect funds and disseminate their ideas.

Dring those years in particular (1889-1897), Ahad Ha'am expanded and developed his theory of Zionism, known as "Spiritual Zionism" or "Ahad-Ha'amism." He held that the most immediate work lay in the preparation of the public mind for Hibbat Zion by means of national education for young people and the spreading of a knowledge of the Hebrew language and literature among young and old. At that time companies were established for Hebrew publications. The *Sifriat Agora* (Penny Library) was established and also the *Ahiassaf Company*. The *Tushia* Library came later. The first "modernized Hebrew classes" were established at which Hebrew was taught as a living language through the medium of Hebrew. Hebrew-speaking societies were established, such as *Safa Berura* (Clear Speech) and *Sefatenu Itanu* (Our Language Remains). In Palestine, Ben Yehuda was campaigning for the reestablishment of Hebrew as a vernacular. His journals, *Hatzvi, Haor* and *Hashkafa,* gave a new trend to Hebrew style, as befitted a living spoken language. Pines, Yellin and Grazovsky were preparing text books for schools in which Hebrew was both the spoken language and the medium of instruction. Zeev Yavetz published his brochures, entitled *Haaretz, Pri-Haaretz* and *Geon*

Haaretz, in which he linked the love of Zion with the conservative yet intellectual attitude of Pines, thereby laying the foundations of the later Zionist party, Mizrachi. And there were a host of others.

Ussishkin participated in all the cultural activities of his own town. He urged the establishment of modernized Hebrew classes and a Hebrew and national library. He subscribed to *Ahiassaf.* There was not a single cultural activity of the Hovevei Zion in which he did not participate. But that did not satisfy him. He feared that Jews might engage too much in literature (in which they had specialized for two thousand years) without any large-scale activity and without spiritual exaltation deriving from a lofty ideal. In that case, the Hibbat Zion movement would reach a condition of absolute atrophy, as he wrote in a letter to Ahad Ha'am which the latter quoted in his essay, "The Inner Torah," without mentioning the name of the correspondent. Ussishkin feared the "Day of Trifles" when every great ideal declines. As early as 1890, before the Committee of the Hovevei Zion had been established in Odessa, Ussishkin had accused Lilienblum of "cowardice." And when the Committee was established he charged Lilienblum with being excessively formalist and too cautious about its official rules and regulations, for fear that the Government would dissolve it. He demanded that the Committee engage in large-scale activities; if the Committee continued along its downward path, as it had while headed by the aged and ailing Pinsker, and particularly during the days of Abraham Gruenberg who replaced Pinsker as chairman in 1892, the whole business was not worthwhile. The

"Day of Trifles" of the Hovevei Zion would not attract either youth or the intellectuals without whom no popular national movement could ever be possible.

And then, in 1896, Herzl published his "Jewish State," and the Day of Trifles became the Day of Great Deeds almost overnight.

Most of the Hovevei Zion were astounded by the daring of Herzl's little book, which expressed the longings of all the Hovevei Zion in bold terms. They feared that the very name, "The Jewish State," might exert a harmful effect on their small but never-ceasing settlement activity. For this reason, they opposed Herzl and his entire approach, in which even the name "Hibbat Zion" was replaced by the new term "Zionism" that had been coined by Nathan Birnbaum. In addition, Ahad Ha'am and the Bnei Moshe, of which Ussishkin was a member, opposed Herzl because the basis of his Zionism was not the historical yearning for the land of the past and the homeland of Jewish culture. Not the Jewish State but a State for the Jews was Herzl's goal, and so he overlooked the historic link between the past and the future of the Jewish people.

There was another point. Herzl believed that the State for the Jews had to be created in advance by a great political-cum-diplomatic step and should only then be followed by large-scale Jewish settlement. Ahad Ha'am and his disciples, on the other hand, looked forward to the Jewish State only as the final stage resulting from settlement and a period of cultural and educational training extending over generations.

Ussishkin, who was both a Zionist romantic and a practical Zionist, found that his attitude resembled that of the Hovevei Zion, Ahad Ha'am and their group. In this sense, but solely and exclusively in this sense, he was always in opposition to Herzl. But with his aspirations for large-scale action he immediately realized that something of outstanding importance had happened to the Jewish people through Herzl's summons and that nothing but a Zionist Congress could convert the small-scale Hibbat Zion, which was restricted to romantic circles of East European Jews, into a large and broad popular movement, capable of delivering the Jewish national movement from the pettiness into which it had declined on account of small-scale philanthropic settlement. For this reason, Ussishkin, unlike most of the Hovevei Zion, adopted a positive attitude toward Herzl and the Congress, though he did not agree to pure political Zionism which had no particular sympathy either for practical work in Palestine or for cultural work in the Diaspora.

Even prior to the First Congress, when Ussishkin was in Western Europe in 1896 to participate in a Paris conference regarding the establishment of Beer Tuvia, he made the acquaintance of Nordau. He also visited Vienna where he met Herzl who made a great impression upon him. Ussishkin saw a leader in him—young, it is true, and a stranger to the spiritual heritage of the nation—but a leader on a large scale with vast powers of influence. And he was one of the first to support Herzl and persuade the Hovevei Zion Committee to send a delegate to the First Congress, in which he himself also participated. Ahad Ha'am was also there. But whereas Ahad Ha'am came to Basle as a guest, "in order to save whatever can still be saved" (as he said to me in so many words on that occasion), Ussishkin came there as an active comrade, even though he was opposed to purely political Zionism.

When the time came to formulate the Basle Program, there was a great conflict between the complete Herzlians, the pure political Zionists, who demanded a clear and unequivocal formulation of the final Zionist aim in the spirit of Herzl, and the practical and spiritual Zionists, who stood closer to the Hovevei Zion and Ahad Ha'am. The latter called for caution in the formula, in order to cause no harm to the existent Yishuv by expressions liable to annoy the Turkish Government. Ussishkin supported the latter; for this reason, the enthusiastic younger men found him unsuitable to head the Russian Zionists, and Dr. Jacob Cohen-Bernstein was elected in his place. At the Second Congress in 1898, however, Ussishkin was elected to the Greater Actions Committee of the Zionist Organization, and remained a member of that body all his life. When the Zionist Organization was established in Russia, prior to the Third Congress in 1899, and divided into districts in order to facilitate its activites in the world's largest Jewish community, Ussishkin headed the Ekaterinoslav region.

Thus began the great day not only of Russian Zionism, but also of Ussishkin himself. He became one of the most active and influential figures within political Zionism in general, and Russian Zionism in particular. He participated in every Zionist Congress with the exception of the Sixth, at the time of which he was in Palestine, as we

The Beginning of Political Zionism

shall see below. There was not a Zionist undertaking, a Zionist idea or a national activity, in which Ussishkin was not one of the leading spokesmen and leading workers.

Ussishkin's Zionist activity as "representative" of the Ekaterinoslav district was variegated and many-sided. He engaged in general Zionist propaganda, in extensive and far-reaching educational and cultural work, in the sale of Zionist Shekalim and shares of the "Jewish Colonial Trust," and in the collection of funds for the settlement work of the Hovevei Zion Committee in Odessa. Yet the center of gravity in all his activity always remained practical work.

I remember that at the First Congress Ussishkin opposed Herzl's demands that the political and diplomatic side of Zionism be stressed and that we state in so many words that until we received full political rights secured by international law in Palestine, we must not engage in petty settlement work or the introduction of immigrants into Palestine by any possible methods. Ussishkin did not succeed. The Basle Program does, it is true, represent a compromise, but the political aspect of Zionism tends to be stressed in it. Ussishkin was deeply disturbed by this, and when the Congress reached its close and Dr. M. Mandelstamm congratulated "our great leader, Dr. Herzl," the entire Congress burst into enthusiastic applause the like of which had not been seen, but Ussishkin, who had been appointed Hebrew Secretary, stood on the platform facing Herzl and did not even clap. It is not important whether he was right or not in his attitude towards Herzl, or his political views. What is important is that, since he did not agree with Herzl on a matter of principle, he had the courage to show Herzl and the whole Congress that he was dissatisfied.

Yet, despite his opposition and dissatisfaction, he never withdrew from Zionist activity. Ussishkin always acted in accordance with Congress resolutions, even if they were opposed to his own views. And despite all his possibly excessive faith in the advantages of practical work, which he always regarded as more important than the bare bones of politics and diplomacy conducted without any real and firm foundation, he esteemed Herzl's political vision and the veritable genius he revealed in organizing the masses and creating great political slogans which attracted hundreds of thousands of enthusiastic followers.

The same thing applied to his attitude towards Ahad Ha'am and Spiritual Zionism. He participated in every educational and cultural activity, as has been said. But at the same time, he always feared that this spirituality, which decried the value of practical action and of concrete work, would lead to the Zionist idea's becoming little more than a subject for abstract thought. Settlement, he held, must precede both politics and culture, despite the importance of these two factors in his eyes and his steady activities on their behalf.

V

The Minsk Conference

THE ZIONIST ACTIVITY WHICH SPREAD FAR AND WIDE after the First Congress was one of societies and circles. It was only natural that each society and circle should go its own way, thus leading to a state of disunion throughout the Zionist Organization. Ussishkin, who always wished for unity and concentration and held that the entire strength of the movement must lie in its unity, spoke at the Fifth Congress in 1901 on a united organization without any room for societies and circles as units. Many of the delegates saw the advantages which would derive from Ussishkin's proposal, but it was hard to put the suggestion into practice. Had it been passed, it is possible that we would have had an Organization far more united than it has been or is now.

But at the same Fifth Congress, Ussishkin's resolution for establishing the Anglo-Palestine Company as a branch of the Jewish Colonial Trust was passed. And when he returned from the Congress, he called a conference of Zionists in the Caucasus, since the latter region came within his area as representative of the Ekaterinoslav district. This was the first time a Zionist leader paid attention to a section of Oriental Jewry, who differed so much in language and custom from the Jews of Russia.

Meanwhile, Ussishkin did not neglect his practical work for the Hovevei Zion Committee in Odessa; he raised money for it, and followed with particular attention all the settlement work conducted by it in Palestine. When a crisis came about in the Yishuv through the non-Zionist officials of Baron Rothschild, and the Hovevei Zion Committee chose a delegation of five members to visit the Baron in Paris and persuade him to change the methods which his officials had introduced, Ussishkin was one of the five. Another was Ahad Ha'am. At this meeting with the Baron, in May 1901, the latter stated that the settlement of Palestine was his own private affair and that no person, no farmers and so societies (hence not the Hovevei Zion Society of Odessa) had any right to intervene. That is, it was purely his private hobby and there was no national or communal consideration involved. Ahad Ha'am demanded that the delegation protest strongly against this view and stress the general national aspect of the new settlement work and its ultimate political and cultural aim, even though this might involve the risk of the Baron's withdrawing from all his activities in the purchase of land, establishment of settlements and support of farmers. Ussishkin's practical sense made him fear this. He felt that the withdrawal of Baron de Rothschild from settlement activity would mean a catastrophe for the whole national work; that the Zionist movement of the period lacked the material means to maintain and continue it. Ussishkin's realistic viewpoint outweighed Ahad Ha'am's idealistic attitude.

It was more than a year later that Ussishkin delivered an address on "Organization" at the great meeting of Russian Zionists known as the Minsk Conference, held on August 22nd to 28th, 1902. This address consisted of two parts. The first was a sort of supplement to Ussishkin's proposal at the Fifth Congress: the Zionist Societies should not be the real basis of the Zionist Organization, but should be replaced by the "Committee of Shekel-payers." The first hundred shekel-payers should elect five members as the local Zionist Committee; every further hundred should elect one more member, with a maximum of twenty-three committee members corresponding to the membership of the Lesser Sanhedrin of Talmudic times. Each district should be headed by a district representative elected by the local agreements, which should meet for a "district gathering" once in six months. Each region, in turn, should be headed by a regional representative elected by a regional gathering held once a year. The local committees, district and regional representatives should conduct all Zionist activities, supervision of which should be divided among the regional representatives.

At this point, there was an interesting innovation: "Spiritual national work should be entrusted to two representatives." There were already sharp divergences between orthodox and secularist Zionists. The cultural question had loomed high at the Fifth Congress, leading to the creation of the "Democratic Faction" on the one hand and the "Mizrachi" on the other. Ussishkin, from his practical viewpoint, saw no other solution for cultural activity save that it should be entrusted to two representatives, one orthodox and the other secularist. On this occasion his views were the same as those of Ahad Ha'am who had proposed two cultural committees for cultural work in the spirit of the orthodox and in that of the secularists respectively.

There was, however, something even newer in this address. Ussishkin urged that "single young men unhampered by marriage or career" become Zionist pioneers. He spoke with great enthusiasm on the need for "youth with fresh strength and a holy love of their people" who would be "at the disposal of the people which would provide all their requirements and who should engage in the holy task for one year or two and do all they are told." For "as long as we have no such persons in the flower of their youth, free from every other responsibility and worry, our work must be weak, since each and every one of us is also engaged in his own affairs." In order that we may make considerable strides forward, it is necessary for us to have a "camp of Jewish heroes." Ussishkin proposed that this group should be called Bnei Akiba (the Sons of Akiba) in memory of the national hero and great teacher, Rabbi Akiba ben Joseph.

This was the first call to young Jews to serve as pioneers (halutzim) in the revival work. The name Bnei Akiba, it is true, was taken up only after many years had passed, and then by a religious Zionist group. But the basic idea that young men, prepared to devote their lives to the work of revival, ought to serve like soldiers for a year or two and perform any work which the Zionist idea and settlement in Palestine required—this idea, as we shall see later, led to the Second Aliyah of workers and "Shomrim," almost a decade before the First World War. And it was this idea which has been the cornerstone of the Zionist Halutz movement from the close of the War of 1914-18 until the present day.

VI

Organizing the Yishuv

O<small>N THE LAST DAY OF</small> P<small>ASSOVER</small> 5633 <small>AND THE DAY</small> following (April 6-7, 1903), the Kishineff pogrom broke out and shook the whole Jewish world, besides having repercussions in the political world at large. Bialik, the Jewish national poet, wrote a poem called, "The Burden of Nemirov." (The name should have been "The Burden of Kishineff," but was altered on account of the Russian censorship to that of Nemirov, a town in the Ukraine where a whole series of unparalleled Cossack massacres of Jews had commenced in 1648.) The title of the poem was later changed to "In the City of Slaughter." Published in Hebrew and Yiddish, it had a tremendous effect on Jewish feeling and public opinion.

Herzl, hurt to his inmost being by the pogrom, resolved to visit the Russian Premier, Count Plehve, despite the fact that the latter was regarded as "the executioner of the Kishineff Jews," in order to obtain from him a promise that he would support Zionist aspirations at Constantinople. At the same time, Herzl began to conduct secret negotiations with the British Foreign Office regarding Uganda. Ussishkin was also shaken to his very core by the Kishineff pogrom, and hastened to the town in order to see with his own eyes what had happened. The great question before him was the next thing to do. It was certainly necessary to purchase land and send the children of Zionists to the Land of Israel with their mothers, in order that their fathers could follow them. But Ussishkin felt that all such steps were insufficient. Such a catastrophe in Jewish life called for some large-scale measure. Herzl felt the same way, and indeed did something outstanding by visiting Plehve and negotiating with Great Britain.

Of the latter step Ussishkin knew nothing until after the Sixth Congress, and meanwhile he was more or less disappointed with the diplomatic activities of Herzl. At the same time, Ahad Ha'am and a group of associated writers proclaimed that "the salvation of Israel will not come from the diplomats" and that a State could not be built on a Charter, which can only be the ceiling and roof of a political organism; the establishment of a State and its basis and foundations must be slow and gradual settlement. On the other hand, Herzl's meeting in Palestine with Kaiser Wilhelm II of Germany had not borne any fruit; the negotiations with Turkey might as well have been conducted "with a stone wall," as Herzl himself confessed, while, as for Plehve's promise, Ussishkin did not believe in it. Nor did other outstanding Zionists in Russia, many of whom complained bitterly against Herzl for conducting negotiations with "the executioner."

What was to be done? What great step could be taken which might deserve to be regarded as balancing the Kishineff catastrophe?

Ussishkin, the Hovev Zion for whom practical work in Palestine and cultural work in both Palestine and the Diaspora were as important as political and diplomatic activities, if not more so—Ussishkin decided to turn to Palestine and take his great step there. It was to be a step simultaneously organizational, economic and cultural in character. And in order that it should prove effective, the step had to be taken during the Sixth Zionist Congress. It would be one Congress coinciding with another, a great gathering in the Land of Israel parallel with the great gathering at Basle.

But Ussishkin recognized the force of discipline. He did not propose to do anything by himself. And so he went to Vienna, saw Herzl, told him of the state of mind of Russian Jewry, and received Herzl's approval of his journey to and activities in Palestine. Herzl spoke to Ussishkin about Jewish settlement in Mesopotamia (the present Iraq), to which the Sultan had agreed. But Ussishkin was opposed; Zionists, said he, might undertake settlement activities solely and exclusively in Palestine. Herzl told Usishkin nothing whatever about the Uganda project.

Ussishkin's visit to Palestine—his second—lasted four months. Soon after his arrival in Jaffa, he issued a circular letter on a convention for the organization of the Palestine Yishuv. In it he pointed out that "there is already a fair total of active forces which have gathered together here from all the lands of the Diaspora." This "is the vital cell which will develop and sprout." It was, however, a misfortune that this cell was composed of Ashkenazim, Sephardim, Yemenite, Persian, Georgian, Bucharian and Moroccan Jews, possessing a multiplicity of institutions fighting against one another, and that there was no unity in this variegated population. It had to be organized as "the Jewish Community in the Land of Israel," a united and unified group. This was the purpose of the great convention at Zichron Jacob to which would come the elected representatives of all the Jews of the country without distinction, and in which membership could be claimed by every Jew "who lives by the toil of his hands and is not supported by charity."

It was precisely on Ussishkin's fortieth birthday that the convention began. Ussishkin delivered the opening speech, stressing the urgent necessity of a centre for the Jewish people, and pointing out how much such a centre depended on the new organization of the Jews of Palestine. That alone would bring us to the objective which our nation has had in view ever since it was exiled. The objective remained the same as ever, but the means had changed. And, said Ussishkin, "A nation whose objectives fluctuate according to the requirements of different periods can be compared with a tree that has many branches but rotten roots. A nation whose objectives and the means by which it hopes to attain them do not change is like a tree that possesses roots but no branches. A nation that is alive and proposes to go on living always has one objective. But the means which it employs must change according to the times." Now it was necessary "to establish a centre which would restore life to slumbering forces." And despite the opposition to any such general organizational body from various quarters, "the required centre will be established and come into being," for "there is nothing that can withstand the human will"—the maxim which was most frequently heard from Ussishkin.

He not only delivered the opening speech but also gave a detailed address on "The Organization of the Yishuv." He called for "the establishment of some higher institution trusted by all and with authority recognized by all, which should be able to unite all the separate limbs of our large communal body in the land of our fathers." To this end it was necessary that every year, at the end of summer, the convention should meet following election of its members by every man and woman aged eighteen or over who is resident in the Land of Israel for not less than one year, who is not supported by charity and who pays a franc a year to the organization fund.

Fifty members would elect one representative to the convention, while any elector, male or female, over the age of twenty may be elected. The convention would elect an Executive Council, the number of whose members should amount to twenty-three. "In this way we shall have a Lesser Sanhedrin, and let us hope that in the course of time we shall also possess a Great Sanhedrin" in its appointed place. Among other functions, this Executive Council would have the great task "of making the Hebrew language a current vernacular in the country."

At the Zichron Jacob convention two important things happened in addition to the discussion of organization for which it was called. To begin with, the whole conference was conducted in Hebrew, which was a novelty in the Land of Israel of those days. Secondly, the right of electing or being elected was given to women, a matter which was a subject of considerable dispute as late as the General Assembly of the Temporary Committee (Vaad Leumi) and the Jewish National Council twenty years ago. Ussishkin supported the granting of votes for women, quoting the old legend that when Israel went into Exile "Abraham came and received no response; Isaac came and received no response; Jacob came and received no response; then Rachel came and her voice was heard on high, and a heavenly voice was heard proclaiming, 'Thy sons shall return unto their borders!' "

To this address he added a proposal next day that the Executive Council in the country should be the "Inner Council" for all internal activities within the country. At the same time, an "Outer Council" was also necessary, consisting of representatives of all the institutions abroad which worked on behalf of Palestine Jewry: these two Councils should always work together in accordance with a common policy.

In the closing address, which Ussishkin also delivered, he said *inter alia*: "Even though we may be at the ends of the west, nevertheless our hearts always follow you in the east. May our right hands be forgotten and our tongues cleave to the roofs of our mouths if we do not devote our lives to the well-being of the Land of Israel! Depart, brethren, every man to his own home, and may the angels of peace accompany you upon your way. Go to the places from which you came, and where they wait expectantly to know all that you have done. Tell them that there are still men in the country who propose to revive the Jewish people. Go and breathe life into the dry bones to be found so plentifully in our land. Pass on to all of them that holy spirit with which you were imbued while you were at Zichron."

The convention lasted for three days and three nights, from Saturday night prior to the New Moon of Ellul until the close of the second of Ellul, when it ended late at night. It was an enthusiastic occasion. The street where the convention was held was renamed "Convention Street," and another was called "Ussishkin Street." The organization of the Jews of Palestine became a fact and was in truth deeply significant. Afterwards, however, came the conflict regarding Uganda and destroyed everything. There was also a certain amount of apprehension of the Turkish Government of Abdul Hamid, which viewed the organization of Jews for the revival of the Land of Israel with disfavor, and there was no shortage of police agents and informers in the Palestine of those days. The Federation of Palestine Jews did not last long. It came before its time, while Turkey was gradually expiring and Jewish Palestine still depended on charity or Baron de Rothschild's bounty. But the healthy seed then sown was to sprout and grow and bear fruit years later.

The Teachers' Federation, which Ussishkin founded at the same time, had quite a different fate. In a circular letter which Ussishkin sent in this connection following his arrival, he stressed the double purpose of such a body: a) "to educate and train a generation full of strength and vigor, healthy in body and soul, who will know and love their nation, their land and their tongue, a generation that loves work, that supports itself by work in its land and for whom this work will be a source of life and satisfaction of physical and spiritual needs; and b) to create in the Land of Israel one Hebrew group, one Hebrew community out of all the multitude of various communities now to be found in the country, each of which wins itself a place of its own and fears to remove the stamp and seal of that particular land of the Exile from which its members come." To this end, a meeting of teachers at Zichron Jacob was held immediately after the convention, on the fifth of Ellul 5663.

At this meeting, Ussishkin outlined a common program for all the Hebrew schools of the country, which should be regarded as compulsory. In the village schools, he proposed, they should learn only one language, namely, Hebrew, for "if in Exile we learnt the book and all that is contained in the book," here in the Land of Israel "we must learn freedom and a new life." He added, "Whether the children in the village school learn more or less of the rules of elementary grammar, more or less of history, more or less of science, does not matter. What they have to learn, though, is this: to be strong and healthy villagers, to be villagers who love their surroundings and physical work, and most of all, to be villagers who love the Hebrew tongue and the Jewish nation with all their hearts and souls.

"That is the essential thing; and without it everything is vanity."

As regards the teaching of religious subjects, these obviously had to find a place in all the schools of the country. "But naturally, there is a difference between the way these things are taught in the Volozhin Yeshivah and at a village school in a settlement."

He also called for a uniform pronunciation in all schools. Whether this would be Ashkenazic or Sephardic was not his concern, as long as there was one established standard for all who learn and speak Hebrew.

In his closing speech, Ussishkin told of the grains of wheat which are found interred with mummies in Egypt and which grow again if replanted, despite the thousands of years during which they have dried and shrunk. The Jewish nation resembles those grains of wheat. For two thousand years it has shrunk and withered in the sarcophagus of exile and ghetto. But as soon as it is planted afresh in the land of its fathers it revives and flourishes anew and "there are hopes for its latter end; that the Jews will yet return to their former glory in their land as aforetime in bygone years."

The "inaugural meeting" of the "Hebrew Teachers' Federation" in the Land of Israel proved a success. It enjoyed a happier fate than that of the "Federation of the Yishuv in Palestine." Far from disintegrating, it is still in lively existence, and honors and loves the memory of its founder. Ussishkin retained his special affection for the teachers and their Federation, and always came to their assistance both in word and deed.

THE RUSSIAN MEMBERS OF THE ZIONIST ACTION COMMITTEE AT
THE MINSK CONFERENCE OF 1902

Seated from right to left: PROF. G. BELKOWSKY, RABBI RABINOWITZ, DR.
TCHLENOV, USSISHKIN, JASSINOVSKY, I. L. GOLDBERG; *Standing:* Z. BROOK,
S. ROSENBAUM, Z. TIOMKIN

THE PRESIDIUM OF THE ZIONIST CONFERENCE AT PETORGRAD
IN 1917

Seated from right to left: A. PODLISHEWSKY, M. USSISHKIN, DR. TCHLENOV,
Z. TIOMKIN, H. ZLATOPOLSKY; *Standing:* I. KLINOW, I. NEIDITCH, M. BROOK,
A. IDELSOHN, A. GOLDSTEIN, L. ROSOFF, L. YAFFE

VII

The Uganda Conflict

As soon as Ussishkin reached Jaffa on his return from the two meetings at Zichron Jacob, he received a cable from the Sixth Congress at Basle with the message "Herzl proposes East Africa."

At first Ussishkin, and all his companions at Jaffa, thought that these cryptic words concealed some hidden meaning which could not be clearly expressed for political and diplomatic reasons. They endeavored to interpret the message, to "break" the code, but without success. Finally it became clear that the cable referred to a proposal on the part of the British Government that the Jews should settle in the British colony of Uganda in East Africa, receiving complete autonomy in municipal and religious affairs, and in general with a basis of autonomy for their internal affairs.

Herzl had written in his book, "The Jewish State," that the said state might be established elsewhere than in Palestine. In addition he had opposed the "petty settlement" of the Hovevei Zion and had viewed with favor a proposal for settlement in Cyprus instead of Palestine. Otherwise it is almost certain that this proposal would not have aroused so great a storm. But Herzl was suspected of supporting the establishment of a Jewish State no matter where it be. Further, he came from a world that was foreign to traditional Judaism and the Hebrew language and culture. Hence it seemed clear to Ussishkin and his comrades that Herzl had now found an opportunity to replace the historical Palestine by some other country that had no connection with the Jews, particularly since he had found himself face to face with a stone wall in Constantinople. The faith in the Messianic mission of Israel, which was the fruit of the Bible and the Talmud, the spiritual bond with the Land of Israel which became still closer through reading the books of Mapu and Schulman, were strong in the hearts of Ussishkin and his Hovevei Zion comrades. This faith was enhanced by the far-reaching activities of Ahad Ha'am, who repeated again and again from the time that Herzl and Nordau appeared on the Zionist platform, that Political Zionism did not aim at the salvation of Judaism as the historical and cultural expression of the Jewish nation, but only at the saving of the Jews from distress. Hence it was really nothing more than large-scale philanthropy, whose chief instrument was a policy that had no historical or traditional basis. All these factors led Ussishkin to regard the Uganda proposal as an undermining of the Jewish national mission and a complete and entire relinquishment of the hope of redemption—that hope which was connected solely with the historic Zion.

In this state of mind, Ussishkin remained uninfluenced by all Herzl's promises that "Uganda is not Zion and will never become Zion," nor by his solemn oath: "If I forget thee, O Jerusalem, let my right hand forget its cunning!" Nor did Ussishkin agree with Nordau's view that "Uganda is no more than a lodging overnight, a temporary refuge until the situation in Zion improves; it will influence the Sultan who must see that Britain is prepared to give the Jews what he is not prepared to give them." Ussishkin and his comrades rightly felt that if the means proved successful it might easily become an end in itself; that in the best of cases the work for Zion would be shouldered aside by the work for Uganda, which would be much easier because the eyes of the world would not be on it; that whereas Britain would be prepared to promote settlement work in Uganda, the Sultan and the countries of Europe would endeavor to prevent work in Palestine.

In order to save both the national historic aim and the practical work in Palestine, Ussishkin protested against the resolution of the Sixth Congress passed by 295 votes against 175, to send a commission to Uganda in order to see whether the country was suited for settlement. The overwhelming majority of the dissenters were Russian Jews, those who had suffered so much from and through the Kishineff pogrom, and for whom Herzl was so concerned. Yet they were the ones to leave the Congress as a protest. Many of them were weeping bitterly as they left the hall; Ahad Ha'am devoted to them a special essay in a minor key, entitled "The Weepers," printed in the leading Hebrew monthly, *Hashiloah*.

Ussishkin returned from Palestine at the end of 1903, and in the Hebrew newspaper, *Hatzofeh*, published an open letter to all Zionists in which he described the Congress resolution as a "betrayal of historical Zionism," and demanded a revolt against it; for where there is fear for the basic hopes of a nation, the very soul of its life, all issues of majority or minority must be disregarded. He summoned the Kharkov Conference, held at the end of October 1903, at which all the leading Zionists of Russia gathered and for four days discussed the Uganda project. The meeting resolved to send to Herzl a special delegation of Zionist leaders who would present him with an "ultimatum" calling on him to liquidate the Uganda project. (No resolution was ever passed not to execute the Congress resolution about the sending of a commission to Uganda.) The meeting further demanded that no resolutions should be put forward at future congresses save such as had a direct bearing on Palestine, and that Herzl should undertake to engage in more practical work in Palestine.

Herzl did not accept the delegation from Kharkov as a delegation, but received two of its members, Rosenbaum and Belkovsky, at a private interview where it was decided that the delegation should participate in the meeting of the Zionist Smaller Actions Committee in their capacity as members of the Greater Actions Committee. At this meeting Herzl calmed their uneasy minds by demonstrating that he had not given up the idea of Palestine and that all he was aiming at was negotiation with the mighty British Government, which, if its offer were not rudely rejected, might yet be of considerable utility in helping us to acquire Palestine. Herzl was far-seeing. One might almost suppose that with his prophetic vision he foresaw the Balfour Declaration which was to come fourteen years later. . . .

Yet Ussishkin feared the outcome of the feeling which

began to take root among Zionists, namely that the "Jewish State" was possible outside the Land of Israel. After the Kharkov Conference the supporters of Uganda established a "Committee for the Defense of the Organization" at Warsaw. The Hebrew Zionist journal, *Hatsefira*, whose editor Nahum Sokolow was opposed to Uganda, used to print pro-Uganda articles introduced by the editor's assistants, Yatzkan, Sfog, etc. Further, the paper printed crass indictments of "the plotters and rebels at Kharkov," directed against Ussishkin in particular. The Zionist organ, *Die Welt*, published equally violent protests. Yet Ussishkin's greatest regret was Palestine, where there were many Ugandists headed by Ben Yehuda. The "Organization of Palestine Jews" came to nothing, possibly because of apprehensions regarding the Turkish Government, of which Herzl had warned the members of the organization in a particularly sharp essay directed against "Mr. Ussishkin of Ekaterinoslav." The name-plate was removed from "Ussishkin Street" in Zichron Jacob, while Ussishkin received a highly abusive letter from the colony Rishon le-Zion, pride of the Hovevei Zion and of Baron de Rothschild.

Yet a man of the calibre of Ussishkin was not to be intimidated by the prospect of a hard fight. He continued to conduct his campaign against Uganda or, more precisely, against all those who believed Zionism to be possible without Zion. At first, the Zionist world had been divided, in the words which Herzl borrowed from Nietsche, into "yea-sayers" and "nay-sayers" with regard to Uganda. This particular issue, however, soon ceased to occupy the centre of the stage. For following the protest of the inhabitants of Uganda and the negative opinion of three members of the Uganda Commission who went there, the British Government withdrew its offer. Now, thanks to Ussishkin and his companions, a powerful party began to crystallize under the name of "Zionei Zion" (Zion Zionists). The writer of these lines prides himself on the fact that he coined this name and participated in the difficult struggles of the "Zionei Zion" Committee together with Ussishkin. This party expressed itself in the excellent Warsaw Hebrew daily, *Hatzofeh,* and the monthly, *Hashiloah,* which at the time also appeared in Warsaw.

On April 11-16, 1904, the Greater Actions Committee met at Vienna. It was the last meeting in which Herzl participated, and the Herzl-Ussishkin issue came to a head there. When Herzl asked Ussishkin, "Do you suppose that we shall get Palestine?" Ussishkin answered with conviction, "Yes! And if you don't believe it, there is no place for you at the head of the Zionist movement." And when Herzl said to Ussishkin, "You are strong, but I am even stronger," the latter responded, "The idea is stronger still!"

Such was Ussishkin during his greatest and bitterest struggle for the entirety of the national aim. Where the idea itself was in danger he did not respect even the greatest of men, no matter how he esteemed him as man, as leader and as organizer.

This meeting of the Greater Actions Committee led to a measure of peace within the movement, but it was a state of "armed peace." Had Herzl been fated to live longer it is possible that the entire Zionist movement might have assumed a different character. But on July 3, 1904 (20th Tammuz 5664) Herzl passed away following a grave illness. His great and almost superhuman Zionist activity and the Uganda conflict both served to shorten his days. It is glib wrong-headedness to accuse Herzl's opponents, and particularly Ussishkin, of being responsible for his death. Did Ussishkin fight Herzl as a private person or for private reasons? Was it not his sacred duty to fight the man—though he were the greatest of the great—if he saw him moving away from the holy idea, from the hopes the Jewish people had cherished for thousands of years? He may have been wrong. Yet there is ample reason to believe that had it not been for his unremittent and unyielding struggle, the Zionist movement might have forsaken its historic road for roundabout and misleading paths.

Ussishkin was shocked to hear of Herzl's death, and hastened to Vienna to be at the funeral. Over the fresh grave he mourned his leader with words that came from his very heart and made a vast impression. Everybody capable of unbiassed judgment saw that in the differences between them there had been no personal animosity or private considerations, but a struggle for the holy ideal.

Herzl's place was taken by David Wolfsohn, a political Zionist but a practical man, a Germanized Jew, who, however, knew Hebrew and came from Russia. The Uganda issue faded away but that was not the end of the search for lands other than Palestine. The Uganda proposal had awakened a fresh and dangerous party within the Zionist movement, the "Territorialists." They were persons who regarded the state (or the territory) wherever it might be found or established as the factor of paramount importance even if it led them away from Zion. They included anti-Zionists who feared that the establishment of a Jewish State in Palestine would strengthen Jewish tradition and the historic bond between the nation and the land, and who opposed all Jewish tradition and regarded the historic connection not as an advantage but very definitely as a disadvantage. There were others among them who did not object to Zion in principle, yet argued that the very bad situation of the Jews in Eastern Europe demanded prompt measures of mass migration to a Jewish State wherever it might be. As for Palestine, the obstacles there were too great and Herzl himself had come up against a stone wall at Constantinople.

So the entire national and historic fate of the Jewish people stood at the crossroads.

Ussishkin did not rest. Early in 1905 he called a council meeting of the Zionei Zion at Vilna; the essential nucleus of all Zionism had by that time crystallyzed in this party, which included all those for whom the Land of Israel was the Alpha and Omega of Zionist work, and who regarded practical work in Palestine as the basic principle of the Zionist movement. Forty-seven delegates were present, from twenty-one towns in all parts of Russia. They included five Zionist leaders. At this meeting, the danger of both Territorialism and Ugandaism to the Zionist movement was stressed; written and verbal warfare against both views were considered, and important proposals were made for strengthening practical work in Palestine.

Yet this significant council in which his participation and leadership played a very important part, was not enough for Ussishkin. During the very struggle against the Uganda proposal he issued a pamphlet in Russian entitled, "Our Program" (1904), which was immediately translated into Hebrew, German and English and which opened a new page in Zionist work in general and practical work in Palestine in particular.

VIII

"Our Program"

USSISHKIN WAS AWARE THAT "THERE ARE THREE partners in the political revival of the nation": the people, the land and the policy He knew that if the people were not prepared for political revival it would not acquire the country, and not even the most effective politics and diplomacy would serve it in the least. Yet he knew that without political negotiations wisely conducted by persons who knew how to utilize external circumstances in order to benefit the ideal, it would be impossible to gain the country. But he also knew well, and never failed to stress, that even if the nation were prepared for a struggle of liberation and were aided by external circumstances, if the soil were held by others, its national and political struggle would prove of no avail, nor would its national cultural activities. He said, "I feel terrified when I think that while the soil of the Land of Israel is held by others, this development is liable to occur to the Jewish people in another few decades. The entire chapter of suffering and torment which it has experienced on the long trail of exile that has lasted two thousand years is as nothing compared with that hour. All the greater will be the crisis when it learns that for those misfortunes it must thank not merely its foes but also its purblind friends and benefactors."

Here we see Ussishkin's attitude in a nutshell. This was the basis of his prolonged and fruitful work for the Jewish National Fund. If the soil was saved, everything was saved.

But he was not so one-sided and limited as not to realize the necessity and productiveness of other fields of Zionist activity.

As he pointed out, Zionism had passed through three periods. During the first period, that of Hibbath Zion, the Lovers of Zion paid attention only to the settlement of the country. In the second period, that of Ahad Ha'am, the spiritual Zionists concentrated exclusively on the training and preparation of the nation. In the third period, that of Herzl, the political Zionists devoted their attention primarily to political activity, although the Basle program also called for the preparation of the people and the settlement of Palestine. Yet it is an error to confine Zionist work merely to one single section of the Zionist program. In particular, it is an error to base everything on political work. That was something which derived from and called for the talents and genius of one exceptional man, namely, Herzl. The Zionist masses were left without anything to do, and therefore Zionism had given rise to Ugandism and what was at the time known as *Gegenwartsarbeit* or "current activities" in the Diaspora,* which had no deep-

---

*These were largely restricted to an attempt to gain a political footing within the established Jewish communities.

rooted connection with Zionism. It was necessary to carry out the full Basle program in all its four sections.

Political work was very important since by written and spoken propaganda we could make the nations of the world ready to recognize the right of the Jews to Palestine and the inevitability of the establishment of a Jewish State there. "In my opinion," said Ussishkin, "political and diplomatic activity is incomparably important." Equally important in his opinion was cultural activity serving to increase the self-awareness of the Jewish people, which in turn would make them wish for political and spiritual revival in the land of their forefathers. In his opinion, special importance also attached to the recognition of the Hebrew language as the official tongue of the Zionist movement, and he demanded that every member of the Zionist movement without distinction should be required to know it and to have some familiarity with Hebrew literature.

But most important of all, and overriding everything else, was settlement on the soil. In order to establish a Jewish State in the Land of Israel it is absolutely necessary, first and foremost, that the soil of Palestine, or at least the greater part of it, should be in the possession of the Jewish people. Unless we own the land, Palestine can never be Jewish, no matter how great the number of Jews may be in the towns or even in the villages. Under no conditions might we deprive the present owners of their soil. The only thing we could possibly do was to purchase it by agreement with the present owners. And therefore *it is necessary that the redemption of the soil should become one of our watchwords.*

In all truth the redemption of the soil henceforward became Ussishkin's most holy and precious purpose in life. He demanded even at the time that the Jewish National Fund, which had been established only at the Fifth Congress, should purchase "large holdings" in Palestine, because "the quantity of national land is of very great importance." In his pamphlet he outlines an agricultural policy most of which remains applicable today. It is necessary to purchase the strips and plots lying between the Jewish settlements of the country in order that "the settlements should be joined together and link up into small complete territories, all of them belonging to Jews and all of them inhabited exclusively by Jews." He also speaks very highly of private initiative in land purchase; for if the time ever came when, as Socialists hope, "it will be possible to transfer all land from private ownership to national ownership," it would be easier "to nationalize Jewish possessions" than "property held by Christians and Moslems."

Once again Ussishkin stressed the importance of political activity. For this particular activity, it was necessary to train people who would be able to exert political influence on behalf of both the idea and the practical work. Nevertheless, the essential thing must remain the training of men for settlement work in Palestine. For this purpose farms must be established on which young Jews would learn how to till the soil and become accustomed to every branch of agriculture. After they had the necessary experience, each one should receive "a plot of land sufficient for him to cultivate by himself without the assistance of hired labor." Here we have the conception on which is based the Moshav Ovdim or Smallholders' Settlement that plays so large a part in present-day settlement work in Palestine alongside the Kibbutz or Collective Settlement.

This was not all. Non-Jewish labor in the Jewish settlements gave rise to gloomy thoughts on the part of Ussishkin. If all the fruits of the fields, the vineyards and the orange groves of Jews were produced by the labor of the Arab worker, would not the day arise when the latter would say that "his hands and his sweat had produced all this plenty, and he would feel that he was entitled to demand openly that he should take possession of all of it."

Therefore, "a general Jewish society of workers consisting of spiritually and physically strong and healthy unmarried young men is absolutely necessary. Each member in this group would have to go up to Palestine for three years in order to do his term of military service for the Jewish people, not with sword and rifle, but with plough and spade." These "thousands of young men" would have to offer their services in the Jewish settlements as workers "at the same wage as that received by the Arabs" and "live an incomparably hard life just as the soldier does in the barracks."

The establishment of such a society would have another important result. The link between the Diaspora and the Land of Israel would become "a truly vital bond." The immigrants from the Exile would unite the Exile with the country and the country with the Zionists in the Exile. Such young men would be found in plenty. "At the beginning of the eighties, dozens of Biluim were found among us," and now "we shall find thousands of their like. . . . The heart of the younger generation is wide awake," it wishes to sacrifice itself, and all that is necessary is to show it the way to this self-sacrifice.

He stresses again and again that "in the Land of Israel we are building not a small spiritual centre but a large political and economic centre which will be able to absorb a considerable part of the Jewish people," and points to Belgium which is as large as Palestine and contains six million inhabitants. Thereafter he calls for the establishment of large-scale industry throughout Turkey in addition to agriculture in Palestine, and indicates the importance of the Zionist Bank. He then deals with cultural work. Palestine must be explored, studied and investigated in the widest possible sense. Schools must be established "whose doors are open wide to Jews and non-Jews alike, whether boys or girls" in which the Hebrew language is used for all branches of study. In village schools Hebrew must be the sole language used, while Arabic and one European language should be added in the urban schools for boys. In addition, a Teachers' Seminary and a *Yeshivah* for rabbis should be established in Jerusalem.

He ends the pamphlet by calling on Zionists "to return not to Hibbath Zion, not to spiritual Zionism and not to diplomatic Zionism, but to the combination of all these three currents." And he utters the hope that the Land of Israel and not the Diaspora would produce "that great and mighty man for whom our people has been waiting these two thousand years." He sees him as a "proud hero

USSISHKIN SPEAKING TO THE YOUTH ON SHEVUOTH (THE FEAST OF THE FIRST FRUITS)

THE DEDICATION OF MEZUDOTH USSISHKIN IN UPPER GALILEE IN 1939. THE WORDS ON THE BANNER READ: "YOUR STRONGHOLD, MENAHEM, IS OUR STRONGHOLD"

like Bar Kochba in times of old, and wise of heart and peerless among men" like Herzl in our own time.

He therefore time and again insists on political Zionism as a foundation of the work. Nevertheless, it is clear from every word in the pamphlet that practical work in Palestine is his basic and fundamental consideration. At the time this was natural and inevitable. As long as Abdul Hamid ruled at Constantinople, there was no other path to follow.

But the numerous and vital truths in the pamphlet were not intended merely to liven up settlement work. They were also formulated in order to rouse a new wave of enthusiasm among young Jews, who at that time, in the years 1904-1905, the period of the first Russian Revolution, were attracted towards alien movements. In the absence of real Zionist work after the passing of Herzl and the failure of diplomatic activities, they were prepared to forsake the unimaginative and wing-clipped Zionist idea. In "Our Program," Ussishkin pointed out to them a new road, a new path for Zionist work on behalf of their people, a newer Biluism.

In actual fact, this pamphlet exerted a tremendous influence on Zionist youth. There can be no doubt that, together with the Kishineff pogrom and those other pogroms following the granting of the constitution in Russia (those of October 1905), this pamphlet was a most important factor in producing the labor movement which is known in Zionist history as the "Second Aliyah." Smallholders' settlements, workers' farms, the first Kvutzoth, the groups of "Hapoel Hatzair" and "Ahduth Haavoda," all these derived directly or at one remove from Ussishkin's pamphlet and its valuable propaganda on behalf of "practical work in the Land of Israel." Thenceforward settlement work in the country took on a more energetic pace. What was even more important, all the Zionists became either political or practical, and the tendency was in favor of practical Zionism. That has been the position thenceforward until the present day, throughout all the changes and vicissitudes which have befallen the Zionist idea and Zionist work in the course of almost forty years.

Meanwhile the Uganda conflict was still raging and the time had arrived for the Seventh Congress, which was to be decisive with regard to the entire question of Uganda and Territorialism as well as that of practical work in Palestine. Ussishkin did not rest. Three days before the meeting of the Seventh Congress, July 24-26, 1905, he called a conference at the town of Freiburg, close to Basle, in the German province of Baden. This was the second conference of the Zionei Zion, and Ussishkin was Chairman and chief speaker. Present were all those Congress delegates who opposed every deviation from Land-of-Israel Zionism, and who approved of almost everything in "Our Program." At the Freiburg Conference a resolution was adopted to wage stern war against the Ugandists and Territorialists, and bring about their exclusion from the Zionist Organization. But there was also a positive resolution: to increase and expedite practical work in Palestine.

The Seventh Congress at Basle lasted from July 27 until August 2, 1905, and its decisions were a direct outcome

"Our Program"

of the Freiburg Conference. At this Congress, the Zionei Zion headed by Ussishkin stood directly opposed to the Territorialists under the lead of Israel Zangwill. The Zionei Zion were victorious. It was resolved: (a) that Zionists as Zionists might not engage in any settlement activity whatsoever outside Palestine; (b) that the Uganda project must be rejected, but that the British Government be thanked for its generous proposal; (c) that the Zionist positions in the Land of Israel must be systematically developed, simultaneously with and as a concrete basis for diplomatic political activities, but that small-scale and unsystematic settlement such as that of the Hovevei Zion be not engaged in.

The struggle was a very bitter one, and those who did not participate cannot have any proper idea of it. When Ussishkin began to speak at this Congress, a number of the opposing delegates rose and began to shout him down with sharp abuse, and even with strong threats against his person. For a quarter of an hour they did not permit him to speak, but he stood out against all the shouting and said what he had to say. Finally he scored a complete victory. After all, he did not approve of small-scale settlement on the lines of the Hovevei Zion, and he had expressly opposed it in "Our Program." And on the other hand he supported political and diplomatic activities as far as they were based on practical work in Palestine.

This spelt the end of every possibility that the Zionist movement as such should look to settlement in other countries or engage at Zionist Congresses in the discussion or promotion of settlement elsewhere than in Palestine.

The Uganda conflict was a central pivot, and one of the high points reached in Ussishkin's Zionist activity. At the Seventh Congress, he was elected one of the seven members of the Smaller Actions Committee, and his influence on the movement rapidly increased.

IX

The Russian and Turkish Revolutions

THE FIRST RUSSIAN REVOLUTION TOOK PLACE IN 1905 during the Uganda conflict. Ussishkin was concerned at the time with two things: (a) that the national, historic character of the link with Zion should not be supplanted by the Africa proposal, and (b) that the Zionists should not be so carried away by the Russian liberation movement that they would forget their Jewish liberation movement. Here it is only proper to mention two important facts regarding Ussishkin's fight against assimilationism, even when this concealed itself behind general Russian considerations.

At the "meetings of fathers and teachers" at Ekaterinoslav in 1904 in which both Russian and Jewish fathers and teachers participated, Ussishkin argued, "A really free school is one which gives every nationality the possibility of developing along its own lines and in accordance with its own desires." He added, "As a Jew I have the right to demand Hebrew schools for ourselves in our own language, to be our own property and under our own supervision. I demand that my son should first learn our Hebrew language and afterwards, if necessary, the language of the country. I want my son to rest on Sabbaths and not on Sundays. I do not wish for the freedom which permits me to die a fine death, but which compels me to deny myself and all that I am. You have burdened our spirits and strangled our souls quite enough! ... I want to see real freedom, freedom to live as I desire and to be what I want to be! ... True freedom is found only under conditions of free development in accordance with the specific tendencies and free vote of each nation."

That was the way in which Ussishkin spoke in Czarist Russia when the old despotism of the Czars began to give way to a new despotism of universalists and internationalists, who endeavored to efface the specific character of the Jewish people in particular. This new despotism was particularly dangerous to Jewish nationalism and the Hebrew language which have no state, soil or authority of their own.

In the year 1906, during the liberation movement in Russia, Ussishkin was in St. Petersburg and participated in a large meeting of revolutionaries of all kinds who were followed by the representatives of Jewish parties in Russia. Ussishkin, like Jabotinsky, was not affected. He had the strength and courage to declare in the presence of hundreds and thousands of Christians and Jews that the Jewish question would not be solved by the Russian Revolution; that just as there was an anti-Semitism of the Right, so there could be an anti-Semitism of the Left, particularly as regards Jewish national freedom and the development of the Jews' special heritage. Attempts were made to silence him by interruptions and by cat-calls. There was even an attempt to attack him and drag him off the platform. Ussishkin was not afraid and did not move. He stood where he was like a pillar of iron until he had said what he had to say to the temporary rulers of those days. He was one of the few to swim against the stream at the time. . . .

After Pinsker's death, the Chairman of the Hovevei Zion Committee was Abraham Gruenberg (1892-1906), a wealthy man who followed Jewish tradition, was highly honored in Odessa for his wealth and philanthropy but who lacked original ideas and the courage necessary for a leading figure in a national movement. He died in 1906 when the Russian liberation movement still glowed like coals under a covering of ashes; but a bitter reaction from the Right could already be felt in Russia, and the Czarist government was endeavoring to gain control over the revolutionary and progressive elements throughout the great Empire. It was at this decisive moment that Ussishkin was elected Chairman of the Hovevei Zion Committee, and moved from Ekaterinoslav to Odessa. He retained this office for thirteen consecutive years, from 1906 until 1919.

It was my good fortune to work with Ussishkin as a member of the Committee from 1908 until it was abolished by order of the Bolsheviks in 1919. There is a great deal that I could tell of Ussishkin's activities as Chairman, but absence of space compels me to restrict myself to a few details.

The years 1906 to 1919 during which Ussishkin served as chairman of the Committee covered the period of savage reaction in Russia which succeeded the initial successes of the liberation movement in 1904 and 1905. The Czarist government suppressed every popular movement whatever it might be. Zionism, which the Russian government had previously regarded as a shield against the spread of Socialism amongst the Jews, had suddenly revealed itself during the period of the liberation movement as progressive and radical, containing important socialist currents such as the "Zeirei Zion," "Hapoel Hatzair" and "Poale Zion." There were also the "Socialist Zionists" and all their various branches, most of whom were Territorialists but were called Zionists. Further, the Zionists were the leading organizers of Jewish self-defense against the pogroms of October, 1905. For this reason the attitude of the authorities vis-a-vis the Zionists took a turn for the worse, and many were imprisoned or even exiled to Siberia. The situation of those engaged in Zionist activities in Russia became very difficult, for in Russia Zionism was, after all, an illegal movement, which was sometimes tolerated and sometimes persecuted, but never recognized as legal in character.

The Hovevei Zion Committee in Odessa, however, was a legal institution recognized as such by the authorities. It had its restricted and restrictive fixed regulations, and if the chairman of the Committee and its members were openly to exceed the limits of those regulations, the Committee would immediately have been closed by the Government. It was therefore necessary to find a method of evading Government supervision and conducting important Zionist activites not included within the framework of the regulations, while keeping those activities in obscurity to such a degree that they would be considered not to run counter to the regulations. Naturally, this placed the entire existence of the Committee in some danger. The aged Lilienblum, who had been secretary of the Committee from the time it was established and whose counsel had guided the ailing and hesitant old Pinsker and the weak and easily frightened Abraham Gruenberg, was opposed to any activity which overstepped the clear official regulations of the Committee.

Ussishkin combatted this hesitancy and cowardice with all his might. To begin with he endeavored to eliminate that shadow of Hovevei Zion philanthropy which had hovered over it as long as Gruenberg was chairman. The funds of the Committee were no longer used for supporting individuals, but were allocated exclusively for the support of matters of public importance; schools, kindergartens, the maintenance of rabbis and slaughterers, general support of workers, the purchase of land as far as possible, support of hospitals, assisting the publication of books and newspapers, and so on. It would be difficult to list all the manifold and important activities in which Ussishkin engaged during those thirteen years. Here I shall mention only a few. In order that the Jewish workers should be able to exist on their meagre wages and compete with alien workers, Ussishkin had a resolution passed by the Committee to establish workers' quarters near the large Jewish settlements in which the Jewish workers were engaged on hired labor, so that in their leisure time they might be able to tend their own plots as a supplement to the wages received at the settlements. In 1908 the Hovevei Zion Committee, on the initiative of

Ussishkin, established Ein Ganim near Petah-Tikva and Beer Jacob near Rehovoth. In 1913 it established Nahlat Yehuda near Rishon-le Zion. Ussishkin supported the Zionist Office which had been placed under the charge of Dr. Ruppin. He supported the Jaffa (Tel-Aviv) Gymnasium founded by Dr. J. L. Matmon, in the possibilities of and need for which very few had believed to begin with. When a gymnasium or secondary school was established at Jerusalem, Ussishkin was of the opinion that it was superfluous under the conditions of the time, and might also enrage the orthodox elements. However, we members of the Committee disputed this issue with him and defeated him by seven votes to five. He immediately said, "If this is the majority resolution of the Committee I shall certainly act in accordance with it." And he accordingly supported the new institution. He did the same with regard to the Training Farm at Kinneret, the establishment of which he had opposed. As soon as he saw that he was in a minority on the Committee, he did his best to help it succeed.

During his term of office the Jaffa Girls' School was expanded and improved by a large grant of the Hovevei Zion Committee, and a School for Women Teachers and Kindergarteners was established in commemoration of Levinsky, a very active Russian Zionist who was also a familiar and pleasant Hebrew essayist of the nineties and the first decade of the present century. The Committee also supported the Jerusalem central school, "Tachkemoni," which had distinctly orthodox tendencies. The important Hebrew periodicals published at the time in Palestine were all subsidized. They included *Hapoel*

Hatzair, Hahinuch, Moledet, the *Laam* publications and the miscellany *Haomer,* all of which were aided on Ussishkin's initiative. He also supported "Bezalel," the Hebrew Language Committee, the Teachers' Central Committee, the National Library. There was some truth in the saying current at the time that the Hovevei Zion Committee did more in and for the Land of Israel than the Zionist Organization.

In Jewish education outside Palestine Ussishkin also participated in everything which to his mind was of national value. No sooner did he come to Odessa than he resolved on the renewal of *Hashiloah,* the publication of which had been suspended during the unrest of the revolutionary period in Russia. He issued a call to the lovers of Hebrew literature and demanded that a definite number of subscribers be secured for *Hashiloah.* Thanks to the aid of the late Hillel Zlatopolsky, "Hashiloah" began to reappear in 1907. As long as this monthly, edited by Bialik and the writer, continued to appear, Ussishkin helped it spiritually and materially. He was always interested in its financial situation. It is needless to add that he took a great interest in its contents and policy without, however, interfering at any time with the editors. When the writer came to Jerusalem at the end of 1919, Ussishkin immediately took steps to renew the publication of the magazine. It appeared in Jerusalem for seven years, from 1920 until 1927, under such difficult financial conditions that it ceased publication twice; but Ussishkin never rested until he found financial support for it in both Palestine and America. He likewise supported *Haolam* all the time it appeared in Odessa under the editorship of Druyanov and Glickson, and he aided various Zionist publications in Russian and Yiddish.

In 1907, when the "Society of Lovers of the Hebrew Language" was established in St. Petersburg with a branch in Odessa, Ussishkin was one of its most active supporters. At that time he fought with all his power against Yiddishism, which began to spread throughout Russia after the Tchernowitz conference at which Yiddish was proclaimed as the national language of the Jewish people. This, in fact, led to disagreement between him and the poet Bialik. When the proposal was made to elect the veteran Hebrew and Yiddish writer, Mendele Mocher Seforim, an honorary member of the Society, Ussishkin opposed it; first, because Mendele had not adopted a completely negative attitude towards Yiddish, and the Yiddishists made use of his name; secondly, because Mendele was not a hundred percent Zionist; and thirdly, because he had not entirely disowned his son who had forsaken Judaism on account of a woman and reverted to it only on his father's death.

I do not wish either to justify or blame Ussishkin, but merely to explain the situation. There was no personal animosity involved. But there was an extreme zeal for the Hebrew language and the view that Palestine had room only for Hebrew, while in the countries of the Diaspora, in Russia for example, it was necessary to know the language of the country. There was, however, he felt no need for any third language such as Yiddish, which was already setting out to be the rival of Hebrew and proposed to inherit the latter's position as *the* Jewish national language. The seed that was then sown has since been reaped by the Jews of Russia, from the time of the Communist Revolution in 1917 until the present. Yiddish is now officially the national language of the Jews in Russia, and the Hebrew language is persecuted there together with Zionism.

In 1908 the Young Turks, headed by Enver Pasha, rose against Abdul Hamid, deposed him and proclaimed a democratic Turkish constitution. This great event naturally exerted a vast influence on the Zionists. It would, they felt certain, be easier to conduct settlement and cultural activities in a constitutionally-governed country. Disappointment followed quickly enough. The Young Turks proved to be chauvinist nationalists, and demanded the Turkification of all peoples resident within the Turkish Empire, including the Jews.

At first, however, there was a widespread belief in the increased possibilities of work in Palestine. This belief was held even by political Zionists like Jabotinsky, and Ussishkin shared it. The latter's sense of reality, however, made him wish to know the true situation at Constantinople, to establish contact with the Jews of Turkey, and use their influence on behalf of the political, economic and cultural work in Palestine. At the end of 1908 he went to Constantinople to find out exactly what could be done in Turkey for Palestine. He had an interview with the Haham Bashi or Chief Rabbi, with the Jewish delegates to the Turkish Parliament, and with influential Sephardic Jews in general. And immediately following his return from Constantinople he summoned the seventh conference of the "Association for the Support of Jewish Farmers and Artisans in Syria and Palestine."

The conference was held early in 1909. The wide range and deep political understanding shown in Ussishkin's most important speech made such an impression that even Lilienblum, who had become very calm and unemotional in his old age, congratulated Ussishkin with great warmth. And when the latter said that he was Lilienblum's disciple in Zionism, Lilienblum responded that he was proud of his disciple, and if he had written his book "The Jewish Revival in the Land of Their Fathers" only to gain such a disciple, then the book had fulfilled its purpose. The closing speech of Ussishkin, in which he distinguished between "birth-pangs" in the Land of Israel and "death-pangs" in the Diaspora, was delivered with such force and vigor that he was ill for some time after this occasion. It was indeed an occasion which set new blood running in the veins of the entire Zionist movement of those days.

In 1913, after the Balkan War against the Young Turks, Ussishkin paid his third visit to Palestine. When he returned he delivered a "General Address" which was later printed as a special pamphlet in Russian under the name of "The Promised Land." (A Hebrew translation entitled "Third Journey to Palestine" is included in the Hebrew "Sefer Ussishkin.") The address stressed three main ideas:

First, the Revival of the Orient. The Orient was beginning to return to life. From it we, the Jews, had brought religious and moral culture to the peoples of

Europe. Now it was our task to bring to the Orient the culture of the West, the culture of Europe. That will be possible only if "we unite with the peoples of the Orient," if "we revive the spiritual world" of the nations of the East, and "not the material world alone." In this way, supported by the millions of the Orient, the Jewish people will re-establish its honor as in bygone years.

Second: the Redemption of the Soil. In order to establish ourselves in the country, "a firm position on which to stand is necessary." Such a position is given only and solely by one thing—the land. And once more Ussishkin returns to the example of Belgium, where six million dwell in an area the size of Palestine. Hence he dreamt not of a small spiritual centre but of a large political, economic and cultural centre. Such a centre calls for land purchases everywhere in the country so that it will be possible to connect and link together whole groups of settlements, uniting them to one another and establishing large closely-settled blocks of land. The redemption of the land must be a primary object in all the work of revival.

Third: Jewish Labor. Without Jewish workers there can be no Jewish Palestine. In order to facilitate the firm establishment of workers in the country it was necessary to establish workmen's quarters round the large settlements, similar to Ein Ganim and Nahlat Yehuda mentioned above.

However, it was necessary to consider not merely Jewish rural settlements but also Jewish towns, particularly Jerusalem—the heart of the nation and the heart of the world. Jerusalem must be surrounded by a ring of Jewish settlements; various kinds of industry must be established there, as Professor Schatz had already done in his "Bezalel." The shame and reproach had to be removed from the hallowed Wailing Wall, which was surrounded by dirt. In general, it was necessary to establish a "New Jerusalem," a Jerusalem of which a truly cultural nation can be proud.

Finally, the greatest success in Palestine had been the Hebrew schools, in which the Hebrew language was paramount thanks to the great and victorious campaigner, Eliezer Ben Yehuda who lived in Jerusalem. The same Ussishkin who twenty-seven years earlier had opposed Professor Schapira's proposal of a university at Jerusalem, now felt that the time had come for such an institution after the success of the secondary schools at Jaffa and Jerusalem, and of the Teachers and Kindergartner Seminaries for men and women at Jerusalem and Jaffa.

At the close of his address on his impressions of his Palestinian trip, Ussishkin related that before he returned to Russia he had visited the famous Cairo Museum where he saw a number of mummies and finally stopped before one of the coffins. When he read the name "Rameses II" on the case he trembled with emotion. Before him were the remains of the great Pharaoh, "first to go to war against our small nation. Now one of the children of that small people stood there thinking of the revival of his people." The great Rameses had gone forth to war against a poor nation which had departed into the desert after Moses, "a nameless shepherd"; and that shepherd

USSISHKIN SUCCESSFULLY OPPOSED THE ALTERNATIVE OF UGANDA, THE MAP OF WHICH HE IS SHOWING TO DR. WEIZMANN AND N. SOKOLOW

USSISHKIN WITH CANADIAN ZIONISTS AT THE WINNIPEG CONFERENCE IN 1937

had prepared against the chariots and armed hosts of Rameses "nothing more than a written scroll, hallowed by flames of fire from the burning bush that is not consumed."

The people of Rameses had not survived but lay inert, buried under the burden of pyramids, sphinxes, and temples. "But," added Ussishkin, "my people is still alive throughout the world, and against it thousands of years have warred in vain." The language of Egypt is "obscure hieroglyphs" and interests only a handful of scholars; but the tongue of Moses lives again in the mouths of children and youngsters, "and giveth voice in the streets." Osiris, God of Egypt, is nothing but "dust at the feet of the God of Gods" who lives and rules the world.

"After I had thought all this," Ussishkin ended his address, "I directed my steps with secure faith towards my ship, in order to return to Exile once again and tell my nation in the presence of the whole world: Do not let your hands fail and do not bow under the savage rod of cruel fate. Do not bow your proud heads." Know and remember that yonder in the East the sun shines on the soil of the ancient homeland, and will light up new life for you. Know and remember that yonder your sons, your youths and your old men will forge you a new life, a life of liberty and light. Know and remember that the Jewish people lives forever!"

X

The Language Conflict in Palestine

WE HAVE ALREADY SEEN THAT IN USSISHKIN'S ADDRESS regarding his third journey to Palestine, concern for the fate of Jerusalem found very prominent expression. But he did not rest content merely with an address. To the Hovevei Zion Committee he submitted certain concrete proposals for the improvement of Old Jerusalem and for the expansion of the New Jerusalem which lies outside the Wall. For this purpose he proposed that a special collection of money be organized expressly for Jerusalem during the Purim festival, just as the collection of money on the Eve of the Day of Atonement was then dedicated to the workers in Palestine. As propaganda, Ussishkin issued fervent proclamations, communicated with various leading Zionist and communal workers and persuaded the present writer to prepare a small booklet called "Jerusalem, Past and Present" (Odessa 1914). This was translated into Yiddish by Moshe Kleinman and was sent out to the Zionist masses. The propaganda made a strong impression upon the public and but for the outbreak of the First World War, there would have been very considerable results to show.

What Ussishkin sowed in people's hearts produced its fruits, however. And he himself remained faithful to the bond of union which he felt with Jerusalem, the heart of the nation. He always did what he could on its behalf. After the War he would not agree to the transfer of any important national institution elsewhere than to Jerusalem. He fought against every attempt to separate the Old Jerusalem from the New. When the British Government proposed the partition of Palestine and the exclusion of Jerusalem from the Jewish portion, Ussishkin was one of the leading opponents of the proposal, and the exclusion of Jerusalem was one of the chief reasons for his unrelenting opposition to the Partition Plan.

In 1913 the language conflict commenced in Palestine. The Hilfsverein der Deutschen Juden (German Jewish Relief Organization), which was partly responsible for the Haifa Technical Institute that was then being built, wished to introduce the Diaspora distinction between sacred and secular studies into its secondary schools in Palestine as well as in the new Institute in Haifa. The religious studies were to be taught in Hebrew and the secular ones in German. This was violently opposed by Zionists; the leading teachers in Palestine proclaimed war against the Hilfsverein's schools and resolved to establish new schools in which Hebrew would be the sole medium of instruction. Many of the moderate Zionists did not approve of this struggle which took the form of a boycott of the Hilfsverein schools, and did not believe that it would be possible to maintain new Hebrew schools. Ussishkin, however, encouraged the teachers by "thanks to the committee of the Teachers Union and the other Palestinian communal workers for rising to stand in the breach." He not only spoke on behalf of the members of the Odessa Committee, supporting the Palestinians in their actions and "associating ourselves with them," but he also demanded that the committee allocate a sum of twenty-five thousand francs in aid of the teachers. He asked that this sum be increased after the expected success of the appeal to the community to contribute to this great effort on which all our national culture depended.

In his General Address of 1913, Ussishkin had stressed the need for a Hebrew University in Palestine, and the possibility of establishing it now that there were already two Hebrew secondary schools in the country. As early as the winter of 1912, at the Eighth Conference of the Hovevei Zion, Ussishkin had suggested that the present writer speak on the Hebrew University. The address was given at the large Union Hall in Odessa and was attentively listened to by 1,200 persons. Their interest was not lessened even when the electric light suddenly stopped and the lecturer spoke in darkness for twelve minutes. The Hovevei Zion Committee, on the motion of Ussishkin, passed a resolution to provide the sum of 50,000 gold francs for the purchase of the Grey-Hill land and building on Mount Scopus, in order to establish the University there. The late Mr. I. L. Goldberg also donated the sum of £7,500 for the purpose, and the site of the University was purchased with this money, which Ussishkin had had a considerable share in raising.

During the Eleventh Congress both Ussishkin and Dr. Chaim Weizmann delivered detailed and enthusiastic lectures on the Hebrew University. Ussishkin reported on the sums already contributed for this purpose, and roused the enthusiasm of the Congress delegates with his words which showed both devotion to Jewish national culture and a deep understanding of the political value of a national university in the country of our hopes. Until his very last day he was devoted to the Hebrew University and remained one of the most active members of its Board of Governors and Executive Committee.

XI

1914-1918

THE FIRST WORLD WAR BROKE OUT AT THE BEGINNING of August, 1914. The Jewish people was reft into fragments. Jewish communities found themselves in enemy camps, were compelled to keep away from one another and even to fight one another. The Zionists found themselves in the same position. The whole purpose of their movement had been to unify and concentrate the Jews in one spot—the Land of Israel. They were now forced apart and the Russian Zionist was expected to regard the German Zionist as his enemy, while Turkey, which went to war against Russia, turned Palestine into enemy territory as far as Russian Jewry was concerned.

In order to maintain some contact between Zionists, an office was established in February 1915 at Copenhagen in neutral Denmark. This office proclaimed the neutrality of the Zionist Organization as such, and could therefore unite Zionists of enemy countries for general Zionist work.

Ussishkin felt it his duty to go to Copenhagen for a secret Zionist Conference. Naturally the Russian government, which had its spies among the Jews as well as elsewhere, was by no means satisfied with this step through which Russian, German and Austrian subjects kept in touch in order to work for a Turkish territory.

There was another side to this.

Immediately following the outbreak of the war, Vladimir Jabotinsky had opposed this neutrality of the Zionist Organization. In a Yiddish journal called *The Tribune,* which he founded at Copenhagen, he called on Zionists to engage in political and military activity together with the English, French and Russians against the Germans and the Turks. In 1915, at Alexandria, Joseph Trumpeldor organized a Jewish military unit which served at Gallipoli under the name of the Zion Mule Corps on the side of the British against the Turks. Later on the Jewish Legion was organized in the United States through the efforts of Ben-Gurion and Ben-Zvi, and in England through the efforts of Jabotinsky.

Ussishkin like most of the Russian and German Zionists at the time, was opposed to this step of Jabotinsky's for three reasons. To begin with, he was afraid of the vengeance of Jemal Pasha, the commnader in chief and ruler of Syria and Palestine, who could easily have destroyed the whole of the numerically weak Jewish community of those days. And for Ussishkin the Jewish population of Palestine and the settlement of the land were always the foundations of Zionism. Secondly, when the Jews had been expelled from Spain in 1492, the Turks had received them cordially. The Jews had always enjoyed equal rights in Turkey, and it was not proper that the Jews should be ungrateful to that nation in its time of trouble and distress. Thirdly, Ussishkin, like all nationalist Jews, bitterly hated Czarist Russia because of its anti-Jewish attitude, which was aggravated during the war. How was it possible for us Jews to ally ourselves with Russia, which persecuted the Jews, against Turkey, which had always adopted a humane attitude towards us?

Naturally the Russian government could not forgive Ussishkin for his relations with the Copenhagen Office and his opposition to a Jewish force to aid the British in fighting Turkey against which Russia was then conducting a campaign in the Caucasus. Ussishkin learnt that the Military Governor-General of Odessa had resolved to expel him from the town.

Ussishkin secretly took leave of his family and of the Odessa Committee which he headed, and went to Moscow until the situation improved. It is hard to describe his grief when his hands were tied and he could not conduct any open activity on behalf of the Land of Israel, "the enemy territory." Whatever could be done secretly he did. At that time he also combatted the Yiddishists, who had begun to establish schools for the children of refugees with Yiddish as the language of instruction. These refugees came from the area conquered from Russia by the Germans, and also from certain Russian governmental districts from which they had been expelled en masse by the Russian military authorities. Together with the late Hillel Zlatopolsky and the latter's daughter, Shoshana Persitz, Ussishkin established Hebrew schools, supported the teacher's seminary headed by Dr. Joseph Mohilever and the training school for kindergartners founded by Yehiel Halperin, which had been exiled to Odessa. He maintained *Hashiloah* and supported nationalist publishing companies in Hebrew and other languages. But his eyes were always turned to Zion.

In Palestine, meanwhile, Jemal Pasha was systematically eradicating the small and feeble Yishuv. He proclaimed that anybody found with Jewish National Fund stamps (a form of fund-raising at the time) would be sentenced to death, and exiled the leading Zionist workers of the country to Damascus. It is not surprising that there was a flight from Palestine to Egypt where the British Administration gladly accepted these exiles who were citizens of Russia, Britain's ally.

I remember how one gloomy day Ussishkin visited me at my home in Odessa. He was gravely concerned at this flight from the Land of Israel. I opened the book of Jeremiah and read part of Chapter XLII containing the bitter words in which the great prophet at the time of the destruction of the First Temple assailed those who fled to Egypt. I said to Ussishkin: "It would be just as well to copy this entire chapter and send a copy to the Jews of Palestine. But there is the Russian Military Censorship. . . ."

"Don't worry about that!" said Ussishkin. "The words will reach the Land of Israel!"

And he went straight home and sent the following cable to Jerusalem or Jaffa: "Read Jeremiah Chapter XLII." His cable had great influence. Many of those who had resolved to flee to Egypt remained in Palestine.

In general Ussishkin did whatever could be done at that time for Palestine. He sought all kinds of ways to provide funds for Zionist and public institutions in Palestine. He endeavored to provide parents with information regarding their children studying at the Tel-Aviv Gymnasium, and to inform the children about their parents in Russia. He also endeavored to support Palestine residents who had property and money in Russia, by way of Copenhagen and Constantinople. There was nothing too difficult or dangerous for him to undertake, if it was necessary for the good of Palestine.

When Ussishkin returned to Odessa and the Russian Revolution of February 1917 (the "Kerensky" Revolution) began, he set to work energetically along two lines. On the one hand he took a very active part in everything affecting the national interests of the vast Jewish population of the then Russian Empire. In addition, he took steps regarding the political, economic and cultural fate of Palestine.

Within a very brief period the Russian Revolution assumed an increasingly leftist trend, taking Russian Jewry along with it. Extremist Socialism became more powerful and nationalism was regarded as reactionary. Yiddish, the language of the Jewish masses of Eastern Europe at that time to a far greater degree than it is today, began to be regarded by Jewish Socialists as the Jewish national language. Hebrew, the language of the Jewish past and of the present Land of Israel, was regarded by them to an increasing degree as the symbol of chauvinism and reaction.

Ussishkin fought with all his strength against these anti-national and anti-Zionist manifestations. In 1917 the representatives of all the national minorities in Russia met at Odessa. At this great conference it was resolved that each of the representatives of the various nations should speak in his own national language. The first speaker was Ussishkin, who spoke Hebrew because Hebrew was the most ancient of European tongues. This action veritably had in it something of what used to be called *kiddush hashem,* the hallowing of the Holy Name. To speak in the "dead" ancient Hebrew at such a time and such a place, and what was more as the first speaker there, was something that nobody but Ussishkin would have had the moral strength to do!

In 1918 the National Council of Ukrainian Jews was organized and a congress of Ukrainian Jews was held at Kiev. Ussishkin was elected chairman and had to make the opening speech. He knew that there would be vast opposition to an opening speech in Hebrew, for it would be an indirect avowal that the Hebrew language is the national tongue of the Jewish people. But Ussishkin was not the man to be frightened by the prospect of opposition. He began talking Hebrew. Scarcely had he uttered the first few Hebrew words, however, than hundreds of Yiddishists began to shout, "Yiddish! Yiddish!" Ussishkin stopped speaking; as soon as the shouters had finished shouting he began in Hebrew again. The shouting and yelling were renewed even more strongly. The large hall became a terrifying sight. Once again Ussishkin stopped, waited for silence, and then began again in Hebrew. Once again the shouting and yelling were renewed, together with vociferous cursing, to say nothing of threats to drag Ussishkin off the platform. There were vast waves and breakers of hundreds of human bodies in commotion, tossing and raging like a stormy sea. Ussishkin was not in the least upset. He remained where he was without budging, and did not give in. This continued for three hours on end, three hours of shouting and yelling, of storming and raised fists. . . . Finally Ussishkin won, and delivered his opening address in Hebrew. That is what Ussishkin was like in those days. It was with good reason that he was called "the man of iron."

At that time he was more than ever concerned for Palestine.

Between the 17th and 23rd of May, 1917, a few days after the Jews of Russia had received complete equality of rights, the Seventh Conference of Russian Zionists was held at Petrograd—a meeting which became famous as the Petrograd Conference. Under the influence of the successful Russian Revolution and the complete emancipation of the Jews, this conference dealt with questions affecting the Jewish future in Russia. It discussed the secularization of the community, personal autonomy, minority rights and so on. Ussishkin, who participated, stressed the Palestine issue. He continued to oppose the "Activism" of Jabotinsky and his group for fear that this might harm the Yishuv in Palestine, as has already been said. But he repeated again and again that after such tremendous events as the War of the Nations it would be impossible to continue Zionist work in Palestine at the same slow rate as before the war. He demanded that petty settlement be replaced by large-scale settlement, and called for extensive and many-sided national cultural activity instead of the small scale cultural work engaged in until then in Palestine. And once more, and yet once more, he stressed the necessity for Halutzim (pioneers) and the

Halutz spirit in every form. His words had their effect; if not immediately, then within a short space of time when national and Zionist activities became impossible in Communist Russia.

On November 2, 1917, the Balfour Declaration was issued in London, and within a very short time its contents were known in Russia. Ussishkin, who until then had not been pro-British because of his anti-Russian feeling and his sense of gratitude to Turkey, immediately realized the great historic importance of an express political promise from one of the great powers to the effect that a National Home would be established for the Jews—that same Jewish National Home which the Basle Program had defined as "a National Home secured by public law." He arranged a mass demonstration of Odessa Jewry in honor of the occasion. The blue - white Zionist flag was carried ahead of the procession and was followed by a magnificent motor-car (a great novelty at that time in Russia) in which sat Ussishkin and three other representatives of Zionism in Odessa. The writer of these lines is proud to recall that at Ussishkin's request he was one of the three despite the fact that in his opinion the Balfour Declaration was only the bare beginning of the Jewish State and not its actual foundation. Two hundred thousand Jews followed the motor-car of Ussishkin and his comrades, and the whole of Christian Odessa was astounded at the sight of this great Jewish procession, the like of which no Russian city had ever seen. Even outside Odessa this demonstration made a tremendous impression, and it was reported in the British and American press. This was another of the great moments in Ussishkin's life and work.

Even greater, however, was the moment when Ussishkin stood before the "Big Four" at the Peace Conference.

At the end of 1918 the Russian press published the report that a Jewish ministry for Palestine had already been established in London. Chaim Weizmann was the Premier, Jabotinsky the Minister of War, and Ussishkin Minister of Agriculture. The consuls of a number of countries came to congratulate Ussishkin on his new and well-deserved appointment. Soon after, Ussishkin received a cable from Weizmann and Sokolow, summoning him to the Versailles Conference at Paris where the fate of Palestine and the Jewish people were to be decided. Ussishkin left Odessa and his wife and daughter, taking only his son with him. The journey from Odessa to Paris lasted six weeks, and Ussishkin arrived at the Peace Conference only two days before the commencement of the session which was to deal with Palestine.

On February 27, 1919, Weizmann, Sokolow, Ussishkin, André Spire and Sylvain Levi, the representatives of the Jewish people, stood at the Versailles Peace Conference and stated the demand of the Jewish people for their historic country. The others spoke in English and French. Ussishkin spoke Hebrew. It was not only the contents of his speech which made a vast impression but also the fact that a son of the persecuted and oppressed people which had been expelled from its country two thousand years ago, and whose language had not been spoken for countless generations, should be prepared to rise before these representatives of the great victorious powers and demand the return of the land of his fathers in the language of his forefathers, the language of the Bible which is regarded as holy by thousands of millions. In the language of the prophets one of the descendants of the prophets demanded the land of the prophets:

"In the name of the largest Jewish community in the world, the Jews of Russia, I stand before you, leaders of the world, in order to put forward here the historic demand of the Jewish people: to be returned to our own borders; to have restored to us the land that was promised us four thousand years ago by the Power Above, the land in which our forefathers dwelt and produced a great and everlasting culture from which all the nations of the earth later took the choicest of their spiritual possessions.

"That land was forcibly taken from the Jewish people eighteen hundred years ago by the Romans, the world-hammer of those days. The Jewish people were exiled from their country and scattered throughout the world. And now I, a son of those exiles, come to you in the name of my bereft people, to you who serve both politically and culturally as the heirs of the Romans, and make my demand of you. Make good that historic theft! In addition to the historic claim which we have to our country, we give as further reason for our demand the dreadful position of the Jewish people in the world throughout the entire long exile until the present day. Nowhere have we found rest for our weary spirit nor for our aching feet. Persecution, expulsion, cruel riots, unbroken distress—such have been our position during all these generations in all the countries of the world. And in these very days—when the wielders of the world's destiny have proclaimed the

USSISHKIN SPEAKING AGAINST PARTITION AT THE TWENTIETH ZIONIST CONGRESS IN 1937

USSISHKIN DISCUSSING THE WHITE PAPER OF 1939 AT A PRESS CONFERENCE

liberation of the nations, the equality of the nations, and the self-determination of every separate nation—Russian Jewry, which I represent here, is undergoing fresh waves of murder and rioting the like of which were never known even in the Middle Ages.

"For us there is no other way out than to receive, under your authority and subject to your supervision, one secure place in the world where we shall be able to renew our own lives and revive the national and cultural tradition which has come down to us from ancient times. And where can that secure spot be save in our historic country for which, through all these generations, we have not ceased to yearn, but have prayed to the God of Israel for our return thither. Not for a moment have we forgotten it, just as we have not forsaken our God, our tongue and our culture. We let ourselves be slain for these possessions of ours rather than betray them. And on this very day I address you in our Hebrew tongue, the tongue of our kings and prophets which we have never forgotten. This tongue is bound up with all our national aspirations. At the beginning of the national revival in the Land of Israel, when we had barely begun our upbuilding work there, even before the war, we devoted our efforts to the revival of our language and our culture.

"Leaders of the world! At this moment we experience the beginning of a new period in world history upon which will be set the seal of your great proclamation: liberation of the nations and justice to all peoples. Every nation has the right to arrange its life in accordance with its desires and aspirations. During the World War, in which the

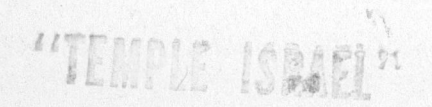

Jewish people also participated with vast sacrifices amounting to thousands and myriads, you aided in the liberation of many peoples. We, too, have a perfect right to request and demand your aid in the liberation of our people and the upbuilding of our country. The moral victory which you have won by your treatment of the other peoples can be made complete and entire by granting justice to the most unfortunate nation in the world, the Jewish people!"

This was indeed a great event in the life of Ussishkin, and one which he could never forget. It was an equally great moment in the history of the Jewish people and of the reviving Hebrew language.

XII

With the Zionist Delegation in Palestine

AFTER USSISHKIN HAD APPEARED BEFORE THE PEACE Conference he stayed in France for some time and also proceeded to England; wherever he was he devoted his best endeavors to work on behalf of Palestine. Only after half a year in the Diaspora did he proceed to Palestine with the purpose of settling there and acting as chairman of the Zionist delegation which had been sent to Palestine by the Zionist Organization with the approval of the British Government, in order to arrange the political, economic and cultural activities of the Jewish community.

Ussishkin reached Palestine early in November 1919 and headed the Zionist delegation, that is, those responsible for the upbuilding of the Jewish National Home, during the three most difficult years of national and political activity. From the first moment the new Jewish political activities met with obstinate opposition by the Moslems, and secret undermining by the Christians. These two factors, combined with concessions to the Arabs on the part of the Government, led to the disturbances of Passover 1920 in Jerusalem and the riots of May 1, 1921 in Jaffa. Riots in the holy Jerusalem, under a British regime! Pogroms like those of Czarist Russia and barbarous

Roumania—it was impossible for Ussishkin to remain calm under such astonishing developments! He protested and banged the table with his fist when he interviewed Sir Ronald Storrs, then Governor of Jerusalem. He also spoke harshly to Sir Herbert Samuel, the first High Commissioner for Palestine, demanding that the British Government implement the Balfour Declaration, aid the Jewish people and the Hebrew language, extend the recognition and use of the latter and no longer treat the Jews as second-class citizens.

This was scarcely likely to find approval in the eyes of the British Government, and the Zionist Executive in London also thought that Ussishkin's behavior was not sufficiently diplomatic or politic. It was, the latter thought, necessary to engage in a policy of appeasement and concessions towards Britain while strengthening our economic position in Palestine. We would have power enough to make greater demands as soon as we had greater strength of our own to depend on. Ussishkin hardly disagreed with the second half of this conception; nobody had stressed as much as he the importance of well-established economic positions based on acquisition of land and settlement on it. But he held that a policy of concession would lower Jewish prestige in our own land, and would thus lead to a fresh spiritual exile even if the area in our possession increased together with the number of immigrants and settlers. He therefore considered that it was necessary to proceed along both lines at once: to purchase as much land as possible and bring in as many immigrants as possible, but at the same time to insist on our rights, and protest against any diminution of them by all the means at our disposal.

Ussishkin did a great deal on behalf of the Yishuv during those years. At the London Conference, held in 1920, he stood up for the regulation of educational affairs in Palestine, and his influence fixed the organizational form under which Jewish education in Palestine is still carried on: namely the Education Department and its composition, the inspectorate, etc. He supported every important economic and cultural activity in Palestine. He helped to organize the Yishuv by setting up the "Jewish National Assembly," which elected the Jewish National Council to replace the previously existent Temporary Council.

Ussishkin was elected a delegate to the Jewish National Assembly by the Sephardic Jews, for he had always shown particular friendliness towards the Oriental communities, and had insisted that the Jewish community of Palestine with all its institutions must serve as a "gathering of the exiles" which would unite all sections of the people. In every national activity he wished for the participation of the Sephardic Jews who have been dwelling in the country for hundreds of years and know its conditions and customs. He supported the Hebrew Language Committee and the various schools. He induced Sir Herbert Samuel to issue the order regarding three official languages which made Hebrew an official language in the country to be used in all Government ordinances, on all official signboards, in the Post and Telegraph services and also on the country's coinage.

Naturally he did not forget what was always the most vital thing of all for him—the acquisition of land. And first and foremost he endeavored to acquire land around

Jerusalem. For of Jerusalem, Jaffa, Tel-Aviv and Haifa, the four largest cities in Palestine, the two latter had Jewish settlements in their vicinity, whereas Jerusalem had nothing save the small and isolated Motza. For this reason Ussishkin, immediately after he settled in Jerusalem, found the rocky tract now known as Kiryat Anavim, purchased the land and immediately brought the first of the new Halutzim there and handed it over to be cleared of stones, to have the terraces on the mountainsides rebuilt as they had been of old before they were destroyed through time and neglect. He wished to establish at Kiryat Anavim an agricultural collective like Degania and Kinneret which had been founded before the First World War.

Here it is only proper to explain Ussishkin's attitude towards the collective settlement of halutzim, the pioneer workers.

By origin, education and attitude Ussishkin was a General Zionist and far from being a Socialist. He certainly did not share the negative views of the extreme Socialist workers regarding the Jewish faith and the performance of the positive injunctions of Jewish law. Nevertheless it was he, though not he alone, who sustained and secured the Socialist Zionists of all hues and sectional groupings in Palestine and established them on National Fund land. How is this to be explained?

Ussishkin had one fundamental principle from his early youth until his last day: "Every doctrine which does not lead to action finally comes to nothing." And proof of this idea was furnished by the history of the Messianic ideal. For close on two thousand years we had had a great and lofty ideal, a strong and radiant faith in Redemption, but nevertheless the children of Israel had remained in exile. Hence it follows that Redemption calls not only for deep faith, not only for an exalted ideal, but first of all and more than all for some action, some concrete deed. The only form which such an action and concrete deed could assume was that of settlement on the soil. For it is not merchants and writers that we lack, but tillers of the soil. Hence the redemption of the land and settlement upon it are the most fundamental of all principles. If the villages are Jewish and the tillers of the soil are Jews, it will be impossible for the country to be other than Jewish.

For this reason our first concern must be the land, and the tilling of the redeemed soil.

Tilling the soil, however, is not so easy. The ordinary mature Jew, or for that matter the ordinary young Jew who is accustomed to commerce, finds it very difficult to transform himself into a farmer and particularly difficult to become a farmer in Palestine. The soil of Palestine has been forsaken and neglected. Here and there the soil is little more than a mass of rocks, as in the case of Kiryat Anavim; or else it is nothing but sand, as at Rishon-le-Zion. It is afflicted with malaria as at Yesod Hamaaleh, or is swampy as Ain Harod used to be. The soil must be cleared of stones and terraced, or else drained. Meanwhile the fruits of the soil are sold in Palestine at a relatively low price, because the needs of the Arabs are few and they work long hours and cheaply. How can such tilling of the soil prove a success if engaged in by Jews with families, or in general by Jews of the middle classes who have been accustomed to a more comfortable life? Only Halutzim, young pioneers enthusiastic for the Zionist ideal and the ideal of social justice, who have no families to begin with, are prepared to live collectively and cooperatively for the ideal they hold dear and are ready to bear and suffer everything and be satisfied with little, will be able to succeed. Only for such idealists will the nation provide financial resources for the purchase of land—land that will remain the possession of the nation as a whole and not the property of private individuals. Even the price of land in Palestine is largely beyond the income of private land owners. But for the nation as a whole no price can be too high when the Homeland has to be redeemed, and a fund like the Jewish National Fund is not a profit-making concern, and its considerations are not those of the private business-man.

This is the explanation of the bond between Ussishkin and the pioneer workers and their Kvutzoth.

XIII

The Redemption of Emek Jezreel

THE FIRST ANNUAL CONFERENCE OF THE ZIONIST ORganization following the confirmation of the Palestine Mandate at San Remo was held in London during July, 1920. The chairman was the late Louis Brandeis, Justice of the American Supreme Court, who had played so great a part in connection with the Balfour Declaration. He and his group made the following proposal. Since the Jewish National Home was now recognized, the Zionist Organization should no longer engage in any specific political and cultural activity. These were to be taken over by the Government of Palestine. The Zionist Organization therefore ought to engage only in large-scale and widely-ramified economic activities whereby Jewish Palestine would develop. To this end it was necessary to introduce into the Zionist Organization such non-Zionists as were also interested in the upbuilding of Palestine. The development of the country ought no longer to be a matter merely of subventions and support, but should be entirely divorced from charity. For this reason it was necessary to differentiate between investment for profit and contributions for work which could not produce any financial profit. The World Zionist Organization should not interfere in the affairs of the local organizations and should not engage in any current activities save in Palestine; it should not even stress the national aspect of Zionism, in order not to estrange the non-Zionists from Zionism.

At the London Conference it was resolved to establish the Keren Hayesod, the English name of which is the Palestine Foundation Fund, for the purpose of collecting contributions for upbuilding Palestine. The Brandeis group demanded that the Keren Hayesod restrict its activities only to non-profit-making activities, such as schools, health, etc., and should not engage in settlement, industry and the like.

Together with Weizmann, Ussishkin strenuously opposed these proposals. He argued that if they were adopted the Zionist idea would be systematically deprived of its national and historic content and would be converted into a business for persons in search of profit; so that it would no longer contain anything of the national purpose and the ideal of redemption. Non-Zionists will never build Zion! (For this reason Ussishkin was afterwards to oppose, for some time the "Mixed Agency" of Zionists and non-Zionists. However at the Sixteenth Congress (held in Zurich from July 28 till August 14, 1929) when it became known that a personality like Louis Marshall was to head the non-Zionists, Ussishkin changed his views and agreed to support the Agency, which was founded at that time.)

In 1920 Ussishkin commenced negotiations for the purchase of the Jezreel Valley (the Emek) with the resources of the Jewish National Fund. The price of the land was very high indeed, and the valley was full of swamps and infested with malaria. There was therefore very extensive opposition to so considerable a purchase at a time when the resources of the Keren Kayemeth were still inconsiderable and the Keren Hayesod had barely commenced activities. But Dr. Arthur Ruppin supported the proposal of Ussishkin who argued that "there is no trickery about land" and that the cost of land in Palestine would increase from year to year, while what was not redeemed today would quite possibly never again be redeemed by us.

Ussishkin and Ruppin won. The Jewish National Fund redeemed an appreciable part of the Emek, upon which we have established about twenty-five agricultural settlements consisting of smallholder villages and collectives, all of them based on mixed farming. The Emek is divided into three areas: the Nahalal, the Afuleh and the Ain Harod blocks. At this important center of Palestine a close, united and undivided stretch of almost forty square kilometers of pure Jewish land were purchased and settled. It is now inhabited and tilled exclusively by Jews. That is one of the finest things which Ussishkin did while he was chairman of the Palestine Executive. And it was not particularly easy for him to carry it out. Despite Dr. Ruppin's support, the opposition to this purchase was so strong that there was a threat of bringing Ussishkin before the Congress Court for purchasing the Emek at so high a price at a time when the Funds did not have sufficient resources.

Ussishkin was prepared to be brought before the Court. But the Twelfth Congress at Carlsbad, held between the 1st and the 14th of September 1921, confirmed the purchase, and again elected Ussishkin chairman of the Palestine Executive. It is hard for us to imagine what our position in the country would have been either politically or economically if Ussishkin had not remained the leader, and if he had withdrawn under the pressure of those who opposed his plan. The redemption of the Emek must be considered the second bright page in the biography of Ussishkin after the Uganda conflict.

But Ussishkin, as a practical man, agreed with one point made by his opponents. The income of the Funds must be increased; otherwise there could be no redemption of the land and no settlement. He went to America in Spring, 1921 together with Professor Albert Einstein, Dr. Shmaryahu Levin and Dr. Ben Zion Mossensohn in order to conduct propaganda on behalf of the Keren Hayesod. His journey was crowned with success. The Keren Hayesod was firmly established, despite the opposition of the Brandeis group to its functions, and despite the fact that the Brandeis group did not support either the propaganda or the drive. Since that time the Keren Hayesod and the Jewish National Fund have divided the upbuilding work in Palestine between them; the Jewish National Fund redeems the soil and the Keren Hayesod provides the means for settlement, immigration, education, health, etc.

In the same year, 1921, Ussishkin was elected one of the directors of the Jewish National Fund. Nor did he neglect the political work for which he was responsible as chairman of the Palestine Executive. This particular branch of his work was difficult and complicated, and roused opposition in various quarters. For there was an increasing and stiffening resistance of the Arabs to Zionism, thanks to the anti-Jewish incitement of all kinds of opponents of Great Britain including French and Italian consuls and priests, to say nothing of others. Sir Herbert Samuel, the first High Commissioner, began to shower concessions on the Arabs at the expense of the Jews, either because he himself was a Jew and therefore felt that he had to be even more than fair towards non-Jews, or else under pressure from London. Ussishkin objected with all his might to these concessions and protested strongly to the officials of the Palestine Government against the constant infringement on the rights guaranteed the Jews by the Mandate. The manner in which Ussishkin carried on negotiations with the Mandatory Power led to disagreements between him and Dr. Weizmann. As a result of this difference of opinion, it came about at the Thirteenth Congress, which was held at Carlsbad from August 6th to 16th, 1923, that Ussishkin was not reelected chairman of the Palestine Executive. This was a bitter blow to him, yet Ussishkin was not the man to despair or leave the general work of revival because of anger at a personal affront that resulted from differences of opinion. He threw himself with all his energy into a great piece of Zionist constructive work.

XIV

Chairman of the Jewish National Fund

IN 1924 USSISHKIN WAS ELECTED CHAIRMAN OF THE directorate of the Jewish National Fund, a position which he retained for eighteen years until his death (1924-41). An entire book might be devoted to Ussishkin's work as chairman of the Keren Kayemeth. Here, however, I must restrict myself to a brief account of those concrete economic and spiritual activities which were of the greatest importance to the Jewish people.

Ussishkin's activities on behalf of the Keren Kayemeth included the collection of funds, the redemption of the land, and the explanation of the basic principles and purpose of the Keren Kayemeth.

In 1924 Ussishkin went on a propaganda journey throughout Europe. The results were a rise of £100,000 in the receipts of the Keren Kayemeth compared with previous years. The importance of this rise becomes still more clear when it is remembered that this large sum was chiefly raised in Central and Eastern Europe which had become impoverished following the First World War, and the value of the currencies of which were very low as compared with the Egyptian pound, then the currency of Palestine. Ussishkin succeeded in raising general enthusiasm for the great idea of redeeming the soil, and hence collected amounts which nobody else would have dreamt of receiving from the impoverished continent of Europe.

In 1927, when he was an elderly man of sixty-four, he made the journey to distant Canada and again succeeded in rousing that by no means numerous Jewish community (amounting in all to about 170,000) and receiving from them an undertaking to raise a million dollars for the redemption of one of the important valleys of the country— Wadi Hawareth, now known as Emek Hepher.

In December 1930 Ussishkin came to the United States. His visit stirred American Jewry and made an impression upon the general public as well. A special conference of the Jewish National Fund in Washington, during February 1931, adopted a plan for intensification of land redemption work by American Jewish communities. If the material results were not immediately so great as Ussishkin had hoped, American Zionists were later to come markedly to the fore in Jewish National Fund work. Indeed, Ussishkin's glorious achievements would have been impossible if not for American Jewry's successful efforts in behalf of Palestinian land redemption during the last ten years. In this decade, under the presidency of Dr. Israel Goldstein, the Jewish National Fund in America has raised sums amounting to $12,000,000.00. At the World Zionist Conference in Geneva in 1939, Ussishkin was deeply moved when the American delegation presented him with a large check for the Keren Kayemeth, and he expressed his earnest appreciation of American Jewry's participation in the work of land redemption.

When Ussishkin reached his seventieth birthday in 1933, the Eighteenth Congress announced the "Ussishkin Campaign" for the redemption of the land. Throughout Jewry in both the Old World and the New, a vast drive commenced in Ussishkin's name and proved highly successful. When he completed his seventy-fifth and seventy-seventh years he again received from America as many thousands of dollars as the years of his age, for the redemption of land by the Jewish National Fund.

Apart from Emek Jezreel he redeemed other extensive and now closely settled areas of the Land of Palestine. In 1927 he redeemed Emek Hepher with money received from Canada, as already stated. Emek Hepher is an extensive and fruitful area lying between the Sharon Plain and Samaria, in which latter region until that time we had had only a few settlements established by the Hovevei Zion and Baron de Rothschild (Hedera, Athlit, Benyamina, etc.). The valley runs down to the sea and was one of the areas reconquered for the Jewish people by the great and victorious Hasmonean king, Alexander Jannaeus. There, as in Emek Jezreel, a number of smallholder villages and collectives were established on the land of the Jewish National Fund, and now increase the food supply of the country. Citrus groves were also planted there and produce magnificent fruit.

In 1928, Ussishkin used the funds of the Keren Kayemeth to redeem the Haifa Bay lands which are of inestimable importance to Jewish Palestine. And so this third Emek passed entirely into Jewish hands: traditionally it is called Emek Zebulun, the Valley of Zebulun of whom the Bible says: "Zebulun shall dwell on the shore of the seas, by the shore of the boats" and "they shall suck of the plenty of waters." This purchase extended the seaboard which the Jews now possessed in the north of the country as well as in the south, and Haifa was rapidly surrounded by Jewish quarters and settlements like Tel-Aviv. For in Haifa, too, the Jewish population has increased, and like Jerusalem it already has a Jewish majority.

In 1930 Ussishkin began to redeem the Beisan lands. These lie at a central point of the country with very fruitful soil, and had been granted by Sir Herbert Samuel to certain Bedouin tribes who had not made any constructive use of them.

Ussishkin redeemed not merely extensive areas and village lands, but also used the resources of the Jewish National Fund to acquire smaller areas in the vicinity of the settlements and the large towns, wherever such areas might be of national importance. Public institutions, beginning with the University and ending with schools, village halls and public playgrounds, were provided with land by the Jewish National Fund on the initiative of Ussishkin.

Under Ussishkin, the National Fund not only redeemed land but also prepared it for settlement. The Fund's resources were used for draining swamps, providing water supply, clearing rocky ground, afforesting unfertile areas, etc. In this way the soil was prepared for settlement by the smallholder villages and collectives, for which the Keren Hayesod provided all that might be required by peasants living on their own soil, besides supporting them until the land produced its fruit and could maintain those who worked on it.

But Ussishkin did even more than collect money, redeem the land and prepare it for settlement. He made every endeavor to induce the Jewish people to realize the importance of the redemption of the land for the future of the nation as a whole. There was none who realized and recognized as clearly as he did that the basic idea of the Keren Kayemeth could succeed only if it became part of the very heart and soul of the younger generation, and of those young people who were capable of sacrifice. The school had to be the place from which the doctrine of redemption would go forth to Jewish youth—the doctrine of redemption in general and redemption of the soil in particular.

In 1927 a writers' convention was held at Kiryat Anavim, where Ussishkin delivered a remarkable address on the political importance of the village. After that the first convention of teachers in Palestine for the Jewish National Fund was held at Kfar Yeladim, the Children's Village in Emek Jezreel. Through this gathering Ussishkin established the basis for activities on behalf of the Keren Kayemeth by teachers and educators in Palestine and throughout the Diaspora. Two years later, during Hanuka 1929, he arranged the second Convention of teachers at Ben-Shemen in Judaea, where he delivered an address on "The Call of the Land," one of his finest speeches on this subject. It was a love-song to the soil and a love-song to the homeland. No book or essay explains as briefly and logically as this remarkable speech the ideology of the Keren Kayemeth.

These are its contents in brief: There are three basic principles in the idea of the Keren Kayemeth: a) the redemption of the land; b) the nationalization of the land;

c) national education. Ussishkin begins with the third principle, which cannot be inculcated merely by theoretical study; for "any doctrine which is not accompanied by action must finally come to nothing." The Jewish people has maintained its existence because its Torah was given the form of practical precepts. "Among our forefathers, education was an education for action; and it was this which raised those powerful generations of the pillars of Judaism, those mighty giants who struck root in the soil of Judaism and piloted the ship of the nation through all the paths and storms of the sea unto the present day. . . . For this reason we must now educate the child to the idea of the redemption of the land by the act of redeeming the land." The farthing or cent or mil which the child gives is not important in itself but is an educational element. "It is not the child who gives to the Keren Kayemeth but the Keren Kayemeth which gives to him; it gives him something to hold on to, and a lofty ideal for the whole of his life." And Ussishkin turned to the teachers and said: "You are not gathering mils for the Keren Kayemeth, but you are gaining the souls of the children for the upbuilding of the nation." That is the third principle — national education.

The second principle is the nationalization of the land and consists of three elements: a) private land can be sold to strangers, but national land remains the possession of the nation forever; b) private land can be tilled by non-Jewish workers, and then there can be no hope of mass settlement in the country, for the workers are the mass everywhere; c) private land causes agrarian revolutions and wars, which may be avoided only if the land is national and not private. For these three reasons the Keren Kayemeth has made nationalization an element of its land policy. Therefore it holds that the upbuilding of the country without national land is not building but destruction.

Finally Ussishkin spoke of the first principle. In view of the political situation in the world, the incitement of the Arabs and the attitude of the Palestine Government towards the acquisition of land on the part of the Jews, there should be no delay whatsoever in the redemption of the country. "The question of redeeming the land is not a matter to be dealt with when the time is convenient but something which is urgent, here and now." He described how much toil and weariness is involved in registering the purchase of each stretch of land; but nevertheless he had succeeded in fulfilling the oath sworn in 1891 during his first visit to Palestine by Ahad Ha'am, Vladimir Tiomkin, Rabbi Maze, Joshua Barzillai-Eisenstadt and himself. They had vowed then to redeem the three important valleys of the country. Four of the five had not lived to see this; he was the only one who had. And the practical Ussishkin, filled with romantic religious emotion, said: "My comrades never lived to see the realization of their dream. But I thank God for his graciousness towards me and say: Blessed art Thou, Oh God of Israel, that Thou has kept me alive until this day and hast vouchsafed me the merit of having redeemed and transferred to the possession of my people the Jezreel Valley, the Sharon Valley (Emek Hepher) and the Acre Valley (Emek Zebulun)."

Such was the "Call of the Land" heard from Ussishkin. There is a kind of absolute conviction in these simple and natural words which must lead to deep thought even on the part of those who do not agree with them in their entirety. For none could compare with Ussishkin as a believer in the power of the living word, of utterances that come from the heart.

But Ussishkin also knew the value of the printed word, the influence of literature with a nationalist tendency; and while other national Jewish workers thought in terms of "circulars" and propaganda pamphlets, Ussishkin appreciated creative work if it bore any sort of relation to the vital problems of the nation and the country. Not only did he assist a number of our authors to publish their works, not only did he participate in festivities in honor of Hebrew writers and poets and support the publication of their books in their honor; he also established the *Lanoar Library,* issued by the Jewish National Fund jointly with the Omanuth Publishing Company. The Library already includes more than eighty books on leading Zionist personalities, important Zionist events, and the development of a number of settlements, smallholder villages and collectives. Small in format but of great influence, the series has done a great deal to extend the knowledge of Zionism and to deepen Zionist consciousness among the youth.

There may be persons who not only do not esteem Ussishkin for the establishment of the *Lanoar Library* but who even object to his having expended Keren Kayemeth Funds on books instead of land. Which is only another proof of how little understanding our public has of the fact that expenditure of this kind is the best possible ultimate source of income.

XV

*The Partition Issue**

I HAVE ALREADY MENTIONED THAT USSISHKIN WAS ONE of the first after Professor Schapira to propose the establishment of the Hebrew University. He voiced this demand at the Hovevei Zion Conference of 1912, and supported the University proposal together with Dr. Weizmann at the Eleventh Congress, which was held in Vienna from September 2 to 9, 1913, and which resolved to commence with the gradual development of faculties of Jewish studies. I have also mentioned that Ussishkin obtained the passage of a resolution by the Hovevei Zion to devote the sum of 50,000 gold francs for this purpose, besides persuading Mr. I. L. Goldberg to make a considerable contribution.

The First World War interrupted all activities in this direction. After Lord Allenby's conquest of Jerusalem (on the Eve of Hanuka 1917), the foundation stone of the Hebrew University was laid on Mount Scopus in the summer of 1918, in the presence of Lord Allenby and the other military authorities of Palestine, the representatives of the

---

*Dr. Klausner's treatment of the partition issue is of course written from the viewpoint of one who was himself a staunch anti-partitionist.

Allies and the religious leaders of the country. Nothing more was done, however, and it seemed as though this great project had been forgotten.

In the summer of 1922, Sir Ronald Storrs, then the Governor of Jerusalem, proposed the opening of an English University at Jerusalem, to contain both a Hebrew and an Arabic Department. Eliezer Ben Yehuda, David Yellin and Dr. Joseph Klausner were invited to conduct the Hebrew Department. It was not difficult to see in an English University a serious rival to the Hebrew University, and there was reason to fear that such a Government University would strengthen the effect of an alien culture on the Jews. Nevertheless, certain of those invited agreed to accept nomination. Thereupon the present writer requested Ussishkin, who was then still chairman of the Zionist Executive in Jerusalem, to use his influence and official position in order to procure the withdrawal of the assent of those who had agreed. He took energetic steps in this direction, and it was finally decided that Sir Ronald Storrs should be informed that the persons invited withdrew their agreement to participate in an English University because, in their opinion, it was liable to compete with the Hebrew University which was shortly to be opened. Naturally Storrs was angry that nothing came of the "Council for the Establishment of a Palestine University," and an English University was not opened. This was also one of Ussishkin's important acts.

Yet all his life Ussishkin knew not only how to fight and prevent harmful influences from establishing themselves, but also how to build up what would be useful and productive. For this reason, acting on the advice of the present writer, he immediately appointed a special committee for the prompt establishment of the Hebrew University in Jerusalem. He himself was an active member. On the recommendation of both Ussishkin and Ahad Ha'am, Mr. Norman Bentwich, then Attorney General to the Palestine Government, became a member of this committee; and upon Ussishkin's own suggestion the committee was joined by Dr. J. L. Magnes, who afterwards became the moving spirit in founding, building and developing the entire institution. Ussishkin was also one of those who from the very commencement demanded that the Hebrew University should be first and foremost a teaching institution, and that research should develop from teaching, not vice versa. Together with Dr. Weizmann and Dr. Magnes, he participated in the opening of the University in April 1925 and was afterwards elected a member of its Board of Governors and Executive Committee. He took an active part in the deliberations of both those bodies, exerting his influence and systematically supporting his national and Zionist attitude. Mention should be made of his opposition to a "Chair for Yiddish," his struggle for a chair for Professor Touroff, and much else.

Ussishkin also devoted much time and energy to the development of the Anglo-Palestine Bank, of which he had been one of the founders in 1902. During recent years he was one of the Bank's directors and participated fully in all the activities which have made it the most important financial institution in the Yishuv.

In April 1936 disturbances broke out afresh in Palestine and continued for three and a half years until the commencement of the Second World War. The British Government sent the Royal or Peel Commission to the country and this body found that the only solution was partition. The Jews would have their own tiny state covering an area of 4,600 square kilometers, but not including a single town mentioned in the Bible apart from a few villages and sites of ruins; even Jerusalem was to be excluded.

The seventy-four year old Ussishkin led those Zionists who opposed this "pocket state." He organized the opposition and at the Twentieth Congress, which was held from August 3 to 21, 1937, spoke against partition in two speeches wherein healthy logic and straightforward common sense were comingled with a deep and lofty idealism and with a vast and ardent devotion to the national aim and the Messianic vision. With emotion held in restraint by his iron logic he demonstrated in these speeches that so tiny a state could not exist because it would be unable to defend itself, and because of the tremendous sums involved in setting up state machinery; further, it could not exist because of its limited land resources and the impossibility of developing industry in it. He reached the heights of vision when he told the Congress delegates of the meaning of any renunciation of the Holy Cities of the historic homeland, and the effect of any renunciation of Jerusalem in particular. "The life of the nation," he emphasized, "is based on feeling and faith." And he cried out: "Do not turn the Land of Israel into a subject for chaffering!" He argued: "The question is whether a living people has the right openly and solemnly to renounce its claim to its heritage in the presence of the whole world. We shall do no such thing! No realistic approach to the needs of the hour, no immediate convenience, no mathematical proof has any value for us. There are limits to realism and mathematics. Two thousand years ago the Jews by the rivers of Babylon took the oath: 'If I forget thee, O Jerusalem, let my right hand wither!' And to this very day no Jewish hand will be found by the River Thames to turn that ancient oath to nought. The Land of Israel is holy. But Jerusalem is the holy of holies."

The political situation in the country was bad. He more than anybody else had stressed how unsatisfactory that situation was from the day he had arrived in Palestine, whereas his political opponents had thought that it was not so dreadful. Political differences of opinion had compelled him "to leave the Zionist Executive; or more correctly, the Zionist Executive had left him." But he, Ussishkin, the maximalist in his political demands, had never been so disappointed or reduced to such a state of despair that he would agree to a fragmentary state without the Holy City and the heritage of our forefathers. "Governments come and governments go; political situations come and political situations go; but our goal always remains the same. We demand the full and entire implementation of the Mandate. We demand our rights and will not renounce even a single one of our hopes."

And rising to the heights of vision, he said: "My great nation, thou shalt receive the land again. We have built across the face of the whole country, as is written in the Holy Bible and in the Hebrew Declaration that dates from the days of our Father Abraham. Generations have passed, times and epochs have descended into the abyss of things forgotten. Much blood has been shed. The rulers of the country have been changed and passed away. Nations have risen and nations have fallen. But our attitude to the land of our fathers has not changed, nor have our hopes and aspirations altered."

His words had a great effect, but did not lead to a victory over the partitionists. A rather vague resolution of the latter was passed by 299 votes against 160, while six delegates refrained from voting. Ussishkin was shaken to the very depths of his soul.

Even after the Congress resolution he did not acquiesce in partition. He helped in the publication and distribution of two pamphlets against it; one being *Opinions of Leading Personalities on the Partition Project,* edited by Engineer M. Feinbrun (Tel Aviv 1938), giving the negative views of forty poets, writers, politicians and communal workers, both Jewish and non-Jewish; the other *A Jewish State* (Jerusalem 1938) containing a poem by Tschernichowsky, two essays by the present writer, an essay by S. Zemach and another by Samuel Ussishkin.

The entire plan of partition was finally discarded by the British Government, doubtless for political reasons of its own.

XVI

His Last Days

NOTHING REMAINS SAVE TO RECORD A FEW OF THE MORE important activities of the final eight years of Ussishkin's life (1933-1941).

I have already mentioned that in 1933, when Ussishkin celebrated his seventieth birthday, a "Ussishkin Drive" for the redemption of the Land was proclaimed and proved highly succesful. I should add to this that the entire Jewish population of Palestine and all Zionists abroad celebrated this important occasion by crowded meetings. Ussishkin's admirers in Palestine published the *Sefer Ussishkin,* a large and handsome volume containing his choicest pamphlets (some of them translated from the Russian), his essays and speeches. It is to be hoped that those of his best speeches which were not included there will soon be published in a second volume. Such collections can and should be used as educational material for Jewish youth in Palestine, for they are imbued with faith, enthusiasm and vision, three attributes which Zionist youth needs greatly.

In 1934, a veteran Zionist, Dr. Pinchas Feldman, succeeded in bringing the coffin of Dr. J. L. Pinsker from Odessa to Palestine in an almost miraculous fashion. Ussishkin, who had taken an active part in this transfer, proposed that the bones of Herzl's herald and predecessor should be buried in the Cave of Nicanor which had been discovered on Mount Scopus in the course of building the University. It was in the same place that he himself afterwards chose to be buried.

In 1938 Ussishkin opened a special room known as the Herzl Room in the Keren Kayemeth Building at Jerusalem. This contains the books, mementoes and furniture of our great leader. Ussishkin had been the stern opponent of Herzl during the Uganda conflict. He who had never agreed with Herzl that the entire Zionist movement must be based on politics and diplomacy and who had demanded practical work in Palestine under all conditions, had always appreciated far more than the rest of the Hovevei Zion the importance of political work. In the course of time, after his views gradually became dominant in the Zionist movement from 1911 and onwards, and political work was at times set aside in favor of practical work, Ussishkin gradually became a Herzlian to an increasing degree, as was the case with almost all those who had been present at the early congresses and had fought against Herzl regarding practical and cultural work. It was he who took steps to establish the Herzl Room and who endeavored to proclaim the greatness of the Zionist leader in every speech and at every opportunity.

Ussishkin himself was exceedingly honored during his last few years. It is possible that he was better known than any other Zionist, being the veteran of the movement, one of those who had created and led it all his life long. In 1935, the Nineteenth Congress elected him President of the Zionist Executive. As chairman of this high Zionist body Ussishkin had a tremendous influence on the most important political and economic resolutions of the Zionist Organization. His speeches at the Executive Committee were energetic and remarkable; such is the unanimous opinion of all those who heard them. If they have been taken down completely and correctly, the time will undoubtedly come for publishing them. That is impossible at present for obvious reasons.

In 1937 the Tel-Aviv Municipal Council elected Ussishkin an honorary citizen of the first all-Jewish city. Early in 1939, a Round Table Conference on Palestine was held at St. James' Palace in London at the instance of the British Government. This Conference was meant to find some method of agreement between Jews and Arabs. Ussishkin was one of the most active people there. He stood up for the Jewish population strongly and courageously, refusing to make any dangerous concessions and keeping his distance from all weak compromise.

In 1940, with the publication of the law restricting Jewish land purchases in the greater part of Palestine, the seventy-seven year old lion was roused again. On the one hand he protested strongly against the law which not only contradicts the Balfour Declaration but also shows anti-Jewish discrimination of a kind not hitherto familiar in British quarters. At the same time he called on the Jewish people to redeem all that could be redeemed. He published a pamphlet in Hebrew and English containing all the Biblical texts promising the Land of Israel to the Children of Israel, from the Lord's promise to Abraham down to the Declaration of Cyrus. He also sent a cable to all parts of the Diaspora: "Read Jeremiah XXXII, 44."

It is Chapter XXXII which contains the wonderful story of how the Lord ordered the imprisoned Jeremiah to purchase the field of Hananeel, his uncle, at the very time when Nebuchadnezzar, king of Babylon, was besieging Jerusalem and the conquest of the city was close at hand. Jeremiah pleaded before the Lord: "Ah, Lord God . . . behold the mounts, they are come unto the city to take it; and the city is given into the hands of the Chaldeans that fight against it, because of the sword and of the famine and of the pestilence; and what thou hast spoken is come to pass; and behold thou seest it. And thou hast said unto me, O Lord God, buy thee the field for money, and take witness; while the city is given into the hands of the Chaldeans." To which came the reply: "For thus saith the Lord, Like I have brought all this great evil upon this people, so will I bring upon them all the good that I have promised them."

And Verse 44, the last verse to which Ussishkin had reference in his cable, reads as follows: "Men shall buy fields for money and subscribe evidences and seal them, and take witnesses in the Land of Benjamin, and in the places about Jerusalem and in the cities of the mountain, and in the cities of the Shephelah, and in the cities of the Negev; for I will cause their captivity to return, saith the Lord." That is: the promise on which Jewish work in the Land of Israel is based extends to all parts without distinction. . . .

And indeed, during those years of disturbances and discrimination the Jewish National Fund redeemed areas in all parts of the country, in the south as in the north, along the coast as among the mountains.

One year earlier, in 1939, the Jewish National Fund had redeemed land within the ancient boundaries of the tribe of Dan, in the northern plain of the Huleh in upper Galilee, and it was resolved to establish there the "Metzudoth Ussishkin" or Ussishkin Stronghold; settlements, smallholder settlements and collectives in which there would be a place for all sections and communities of the Jewish nation, including Ashkenazim, Sephardim and Oriental Jews, also for all the parties of the Zionist movement from the two groups of General Zionists and the Mizrachi to the Palestine Labor Party and the Shomer Hatzair. That was the last great satisfaction which Ussishkin had in his life.

Despite the fact that he was approaching the limits of human life ("the days of our years are three score years and ten; and if there be vigor then eighty years"), his national and Zionist work neither ceased nor faltered. There was no activity, political, economic or cultural, in which he did not participate to the end of his life. He was still the mainstay of all work pertaining to the nation, the land and the language. At the age of seventy-seven he accepted the chairmanship of the "Council for Establishing Hebrew in Palestine," after seeing the danger to our tongue from the flooding of the country by other languages. There was never a memorial for a great personality or outstanding event, nor a jubilee celebration of a poet, writer or important communal worker, in which Ussishkin did not participate with a speech as well as a grant in aid of the publication of writings or the issue of a suitable book.

His speeches during recent years were unique of their kind. They contained no sounding phrases, there was no shouting or outcry in them, but, nevertheless, or maybe precisely on that account, they went to the very heart and exerted an absolutely purifying effect. Here I shall merely mention the remarkable address on Joshua Barzillai; the heartfelt speech on Rabbi Samuel Mohilever where he tells how the latter refused to accept the proposal of Baron Hirsch's emissary that the Zionists should agree to settlement in Argentine instead of Palestine; the magnificent speeches on Eliezer Ben Yehuda and Ahad Ha'am; the speeches at recent teachers' conferences, at youth gatherings; the speech at Kiryat Anavim on the value of the soil for the nation; and many another. As I have already said above, when these speeches, which are not included in *Sefer Ussishkin,* are put together, we shall possess a book whose influence on the younger generation will be far greater than we now imagine. In them burns the flame of faith in the future of the nation, together with a practcial logic which does not subjugate the great vision but makes the faith more possible of accomplishment and brings the vision closer to realization.

Until his last day "his eye was not dim nor his natural force abated." He was as upright as ever and his bright blue eyes, filled with vision, were still youthful. On the 13th of Shevat 5701 (1941) he celebrated his golden wedding with his wife, Esther, and hundreds of friends and acquaintances visited him to celebrate the occasion.

The Last Days

A few days before Rosh Hashana, 1941, Ussishkin became ill. After he had been operated on at the Hadassah Hospital he wrote from his sick bed a magnificent response to the first call of Russian Jewry to world Jewry with regard to the war against the common foe. His words were read from the manuscript into the microphone by somebody else, and were published throughout Russia.

Between the New Year and the Day of Atonement, his health improved and he asked to be brought home to Rehavia. The day following the Day of Atonement he still engaged in the affairs of the Jewish National Fund and signed various documents. In the evening, however, he suddenly took a turn for the worse, and on Thursday night, Tishri 11, 5702 (October 2, 1941) he passed away in the presence of all his family, having completed his seventy-eighth year at the New Moon of Ellul 5701.

In his will he requested that no speeches be delivered at his funeral, and that he should be buried in the Cave of Nicanor where he himself had proposed that the remains of Pinsker be given their final resting place. This was profoundly symbolic. Pinsker was a political Zionist pure and simple, but had engaged in the petty settlement work of the Hovevei Zion because settlement is what can bring about the realization of the great political ideal, the Jewish State in Palestine. Ussishkin was his disciple and comrade with regard to both these elements of Zionism.

Ussihkin's will was carried out. On the eve of Sabbath, Tishri 12 (October 3), the funeral took place. Despite the brief notification, his body was accompanied by a vast throng. It was a royal funeral. The body of the great leader of the fulfilment was silently lowered into place besides the remains of the great leader of the initial stages, and those present dispersed knowing that here lay buried the two great Russian Jews for whom the redemption of Israel had been the very breath of life. . . .

Thirty days after the passing of Ussishkin the Jewish National Fund executive arranged a pilgrimage to his grave, the like of which Jewry has not seen. Hundreds of people from every one of the settlements and urban quarters established on Jewish National Fund land, came to the Cave of Nicanor, bearing little sacks containing some of their soil. In mournful silence each group placed its sack on the fresh grave. . . . This was a sight which will never be forgotten by any of those who saw it.

XVII

Man and Leader

The passing of Ussishkin meant the departure of one of the strongest personalities which the Jewish people ever had. A faith of steel in the correctness of his opinions and an iron resolution in all that appertained to their realization—these are what made Ussishkin, if not the greatest, then certainly the most outstanding figure in the Zionist movement of which he had been the mainstay and backbone for sixty years, from the days of Pinsker and Lilienblum, through the period of Ahad Ha'am and Herzl, until the time of Weizmann and Sokolow. Throughout his life his was a synthetic Zionism, comprehending politics, economics and culture, three sacred national activities which are one. He did not originate any one of these three principles, but had his own approach to every idea which he received from Pinsker, Lilienblum, Ahad Ha'am and Herzl; and after his own fashion he was concerned with every one of these Zionist elements. There was no Jewish national or Zionist issue on which Ussishkin did not have a view of his own, and he acted always in accordance with his own views. It is an error to suppose that the one-sided or monotonous is great; what is really great is many-sided and many-hued, but always derives from one central point in the soul.

That was Ussishkin. His central point was: "Every doctrine which does not lead to action must come to nothing." This central point, however, did not lead to the ignoring of other considerations. Although Ussishkin was fundamentally practical there were few among us who esteemed political and cultural work as much as he.

I have already mentioned his vast esteem for Herzl and the political ideal. It was because of his Herzlianism that he had to leave the Zionist Executive in 1923. Yet he was the greatest of all admirers of Ahad Ha'am, Bialik and Tschernichowsky. He did more than anybody else for *Hashiloah, Haomer,* the *Lanoar* Library, the Teachers' Association, various Hebrew writers and youth organizations. There were few Zionist leaders who appreciated scholars as he did, who learnt from them and gave consideration to their views; yet this in no way diminished the character of his practical Zionist work. There was not a Zionist in the world whose spirit so absorbed, and was so enriched by, the radiance of the whole vast Zionist idea as Ussishkin.

Ussishkin's energy knew no bounds. The Hovevei Zion Committee used to receive about three thousand letters a year. As one of its members I can bear witness to the fact that there was scarcely a single letter, whether important or unimportant, which Ussishkin did not read and answer, either himself or through the secretaries of the Committee. He was a fighter all his life, and we are accustomed to regard fighting as something opposed to practical day-to-day work with its petty details. It was the greatness of Ussishkin that he combined the capacity of fighting for great ideals with a respect for detail.

Ussishkin could be hard as iron, but there were

The Last Days

moments when he was as pliant as a reed. His eyes would fill with tears when he heard of a mishap to any of his friends, many of whom he helped in secret. Some accused him of hard-heartedness, but it is necessary to know the circumstances which sometimes compelled him to be harsh to the individual for the sake of the general well-being. In national, religious, traditional and historical matters he was an utter romantic, despite all his practicality. Jerusalem, the Wailing Wall, the Prophets, the Kings, the Hasmoneans and the Sages of the Talmud were all hallowed in his eyes, and the memory of them would fill him with sacred awe.

It is difficult to describe all his vast activities. In this small book mention has been made only of his most important and outstanding work. Were I to try to give a list of all he achieved during his sixty years of communal life, it would take more than three large volumes. Here I shall therefore revert only to the greatest moments of his life. The organization of the Jews of Palestine and the Teachers' Association; the establishment of auxiliary workers' settlements near the large settlements; the Uganda conflict; the Hebrew address at the Versailles Peace Conference; the purchases of Emek Jezreel, Emek Zebulun and Emek Hepher, and the fight against partition. These activities will not be forgotten as long as the Jewish people exist, even when the Zionist movement has brought Jewry the full redemption.

As regards his activities as chairman of the Jewish National Fund, it is enough to record that when he was elected a member of the directorate the Fund owned an area of 22,000 dunams, while when he died it possessed

561,000 dunams. As regards its income, when he was elected chairman in 1924, it collected £70,000 a year, but by the end of 1941, when he expired, its annual income was £600,000. This vast increase in lands and funds was something uncommon for a national institution, and Ussishkin was undoubtedly not the only cause of it. But there is equally no doubt that Ussishkin was one of the most important factors leading to the increase in property and income of the Jewish National Fund. As we have seen, there was a time when Ussishkin had to defend his purchase of Emek Jezreel against his opponents. Whatever else may be said, he was the central personality of the Jewish National Fund for about twenty years.

Through the death of Ussishkin the Jewish people as a whole has lost a unique personality and a unique national and Zionist leader. It is hard to imagine that his like will soon be found. His Hebrew and general education amid a Jewry of millions, his deep roots in the soil of tradition, his boundless love for historical Judaism, his fervent Messianic vision—all these fitted him to be one of the leading fighters for the idea of redemption, the redemption of the land and the redemption of the people; and one of those most devoted to the national faith, language and literature of Israel in the Diaspora as in Palestine.

For us Menahem ben Moshe Zvi Ussishkin remains a radiant personality who will serve as a beacon for coming generations in their struggle for our people and the cities of our God, until the coming of the full redemption, the three-fold redemption of the nation returning to complete life in its historic country and its historic language.

Jerusalem-Talpioth, 18th Sivan, 5702.

USSISHKIN SPEAKING AT THE DEDICATION OF THE KING GEORGE V
FOREST
To the right: DR. CHAIM WEIZMANN; *in the center:* SIR ARTHUR WAUCHOPE,
THEN HIGH COMMISSIONER FOR PALESTINE

USSISHKIN'S OFFICE IN THE KEREN KAYEMET BUILDING IN
JERUSALEM

THE FUNERAL PROCESSION LEAVING USSISHKIN'S HOME IN REHAVIA, JERUSALEM

USSISHKIN'S GRAVE IN THE CAVE OF NICANOR, ON MT. SCOPUS, COVERED WITH SACKS OF EARTH FROM EACH OF THE NATIONAL FUND SETTLEMENTS

INDEX

Abdul Hamid, 57, 61, 67, 80, 93.
Ahad Ha'am, 35, 40, 41, 45, 46, 47, 48, 50, 52, 53, 56, 66, 67, 76, 133, 137, 146, 149, 150.
Ahad Ha'amism, 44.
Ahiasaf Company, 44, 45.
Ahduth Haavoda, 81.
Afuleh, 123.
Agency, see Jewish Agency.
Ain Harod, 119, 123.
Akiba ben Joseph, Rabbi, 54.
Alexander Jannaeus, 129.
Aliyah, Second, 54, 81.
Allenby Lord, 135.
America, see United States.
American Jewry, 104, 124, 128.
American Zionists, 128.
Anglo Palestine Bank, 137.
    Company, APC, 51, 80.
Anti-Semitism, 86.
Association for the Support of Jewish Farmers and Artisans in Syria and Palestine, 94.
Athlit, 129.

Balfour Declaration, 68, 110, 116, 121, 143.
Bar Kochba, 81.
Baron Hirsch, 146.
Barzillai, J., (Eisenstadt), 35, 133, 146.
Basle, 48, 57, 65, 82
    Program, 48, 49, 76, 77, 110.
Beer Jacob, 90.
Beer Tuvia, 47.
Beisan, 130.
Belkovsky, Prof. G., 68.
Ben Gurion, David, 104.
Ben Shemen Convention, 131.

Bentwich, Norman, 137.
Benyamina, 129.
Ben Yehuda, Eliezer, 33, 44, 69, 96, 146.
Ben Zvi, Isaac, 104.
Berlin, Reb Haim, 16.
Berlin, Naphtali Zvi Yehuda, 16, 30.
Bernstein-Cohen, Jacob, 48.
Bezalel School, 91, 96.
Bialik, Ch. N., 55, 91, 150.
Bilu, 20, 22, 23, 30, 34.
Biluin, 79.
Biluism, 81.
Birnbaum, Nathan, 46.
Bnei Akiba, 54.
Bnei Moshe, 35, 46.
Bnei Zion, 26.
Bolsheviks, 87.
Brandeis, Louis, 121.
    Group, 121, 124.
British Foreign Office, 55.
    Government, 65, 68, 83, 100, 115, 116, 125, 138, 140, 143.

"Call of the Land," 95, 131, 133.
Canada, 128, 129.
Carlsbad, 123, 125.
Cave of Nicanor, 142, 147, 148.
Chazanowitz, Dr. J., 35.
"City of Slaughter," 55.
Congress, (Zionist),
    First, 47, 49, 50, 51.
    Second, 48.
    Third, 48.
    Fifth, 51, 53, 78.
    Sixth, 57, 65, 67.
    Seventh, 82, 83, 84.

Index

Eleventh, 101, 102, 135.
Twelfth 123.
Thirteenth, 125.
Sixteenth, 122.
Eighteenth, 129.
Nineteenth, 142.
Twentieth, 138, 139.
Constantinople, 55, 66, 72, 84, 93, 97.
Copenhagen, 103, 104, 105, 107.
  Zionist Conference, 103.
Czar Aleaxnder, III, 27.
Czarist Government, see Russian Government.

Degania, 118.
Democartic Faction, 53.
Die Welt, 69.
Disturbances of Passover, 1920, 115.
Druskenik Conference, 30-32.
Drubin, 23.
Druyanov, Alter, 92.
Dubrovna, 15, 16, 17.

Ein Ganim, 90, 95.
Einstein, Prof. Albert, 124.
Ekaterinoslav, 43, 48, 49, 50, 85, 86.
Emek Hefer, 128, 129, 133, 151.
  Jezreel, 122, 123, 129, 131, 133, 151, 152.
  Zebulun, 129, 133, 151.
English University at Jerusalem, 135, 136.
Enver Pasha, 93.

Federation of the Yishuv, see Yishuv.
Feinbrun, M., 140.
Feldman, Dr. Pinchas, 141.

Freiburg Conference, 83.
  Resolution, 82.
Frischmann, David, 27.

Gallipoli, 104.
Gedera, 30, 33.
Geneva Conference, 128.
Glickson, Dr. Moshe, 92.
Goldberg, I. L., 101, 135.
Goldstein, Dr. Israel, 128.
Gordon, J. L., 21.
Greater Actions Committee, 48, 68, 70.
Great Britain, see British Government.
Grodzinsky, Benjamin, 18.
Grazovsky, Yehuda, 47.
Gruenberg, Abraham, 66, 87, 89.

Habad, 15, 29.
Haham Bashi, 93.
Hahinuch, 91.
Haifa, 117, 129, 130.
  Bay, 129.
  Technical Institute, 100.
Halperin, Yehiel, 105.
Halutz, Halutzim, 109, 110, 118, 119.
Hamelitz, 18, 28, 29, 35, 40.
Haolom, 91.
Haomer, 91, 150.
Haor, 44.
Hapoel Hatzair, 81, 88.
Hapoel Hatzair, Weekly, 90, 91.
Hashiloah, 67, 70, 91, 105, 150.
Hashkafa, 44.
Hashomer Hatzair, see Shomer Hatzair.
Hasmoneans, 129, 151.
Hatsefira, 69.
Hashahar, 18.

Index

Hatzofeh, 67, 70.
Hatzvi, 44.
Hebrew Language, 44, 59, 66, 77, 80, 85, 92, 96, 114, 116.
  Committee, 71, 117.
  Conflict, 100.
Hebrew Literature, 18, 44, 77, 91.
Hebrew Schools, 85, 96.
Hebrew University, 33, 96, 101, 102, 130, 135, 136, 137.
Hedera, 129.
Herzl, Theodor, 46, 47, 48, 55, 56, 57, 65, 66, 67, 68, 69, 70, 71, 81, 142, 149, 150.
  Room, 142.
Hibbat Zion, 26, 28, 29, 30, 32, 35, 43, 44, 45, 46, 47, 76, 80.
Hilfsverein der Deutschen Juden, 100.
Hissin, Dr. Chaim, 22, 129.
Hovevei Zion, 25, 26, 27, 28, 29, 30, 34, 35, 43, 44, 45, 46, 47, 48, 49, 51, 52, 56, 65, 66, 69, 83, 87, 88, 89, 90, 91, 99, 100, 101, 102, 129, 135, 142, 147, 150.
Huleh, 145.
Hushi Ha-Archi, see Levontin Yehiel.

Jabotinsky, Z. (Vladimir), 86, 93, 104, 109, 111.
Jaffa, 36, 43, 57, 65, 118.
Jaffa (Tel Aviv) Gymnasium, 90, 96.
  Girls' School, 90.
Jemal Pasha, 104, 106.
Jeremiah, 143, 144.

Jerusalem, 36, 38, 39, 41, 95, 99, 100, 117, 137, 138, 151.
  Conquest of, 135.
Jeshuron, Synagogue, 17.
Jewish Agency, 122.
Jewish Colonial Trust, 49, 51.
Jewish Labor, 95.
Jewish Legion, 104, 105.
Jewish National Assembly, 117.
Jewish National Home, 110, 115, 121.
Jewish National Council, 117.
Jewish National Fund, 76, 77, 78, 106, 118, 120, 122, 123, 124, 127, 128, 129, 130, 131, 132, 133, 134, 142, 145, 146, 147, 148, 151, 152.
Jewish Self Defense, 88.
Jewish State, 46, 72, 77, 140.
Jewish Youth, 26, 131, 141.
Jews of Palestine, see Yishuv.
Jews of Russia, 19, 20, 21, 51, 67, 92, 112, 146, 147.
Jezreel Valley, see Emek Jezreel.

Kattowitz Conference, 30.
Keren Hayesod, 121, 124, 130.
Keren Kayemeth, see Jewish National Fund.
Kharkov, 23, 68, 69.
  Conference, 68, 69.
Kfar, Yeladim, 131.
Kibbutz, 79.
Kiev, Congress of Ukrainian Jews, 108, 109.
Kinnereth, 90, 118.
Kiryath Anavim, 118, 119, 131, 146.
Kisheneff Pogrom, 55, 56, 67, 81.
Klausner, Dr. Joseph, 136.

Index

Kleinman, Moshe, 99.
Kvutzoth, 81, 120.

Laam, 91.
Land of Israel, 18, 22, 23, 25, 28, 32, 33, 40, 56, 57, 58, 59, 66, 72, 80, 91, 94, 105, 106, 113, 138, 143, 144.
Lanoar Library, 134, 150.
Levi, Sylvain, 111.
Levin, Dr. Shmaryahu, 124.
Levinsky, A. L., 36, 90.
Levontin, Yehiel, 25, 26.
Levontin, Z. D., 34.
Lilienblum, Moshe, Leib, 28, 29, 30, 31, 35, 36, 45, 89, 93, 149.
London Conference, 116, 122.

Magnes, Dr. J. L., 137.
Mandelstamm, Dr. M., 49.
Mapu, Abraham, 18, 66.
Marshall, Louis, 122.
Masliansky, Z. H., 28.
Maskilim, 19, 25.
Matmon-Cohen, Dr. J. L., 90.
Maze, Rabbi Jacob, 25, 133.
Mendele Mocher, Seforim, 92.
Messianic Hope, 27, 66, 118, 138, 152.
Metzudoth Ussishkin, 145.
Minsk Conference, 52.
Mintz, A. L., 26.
Mintz, Shalom, 26.
Mizrachi, 45, 53, 145.
Mohilev District, 15.
Mohilever, Dr. Joseph, 105.
Mohilever, Rabbi Samuel, 30, *Moledet,* (Periodical), 91.
Moscow, 16, 23, 26, 28, 31, 33.
Moshav Ovdim, 79.
Motza, 118.
Mount Scopus, 101, 135, 142.

Mossensohn, Dr. Ben Zion, 124.
Nahalal, 123.
Nahlat Yehuda, 90, 91.
National Library, 91.
Nordau, Dr. Max, 47, 66.

Odessa, 35, 45, 49, 51, 52, 81, 87, 88, 99, 100, 101, 105-107, 110, 111, 141.
"Our Program," 69, 73, 81, 83.

"Palestine" (periodical), 28.
Palestine, Execuitve, 43, 123, 124.
Palestine, Foundation Fund, see Keren Hayesod.
Palestine Government, 121, 124, 133.
Palestine Jewish population, see Yishuv.
Palestine Jewry, see Yishuv.
Palestine Labor Party, 145.
Palestine Mandate, 121, 125, 139.
Palestine National Library, 35, 36.
Palestine practical work in, 47, 56, 68, 72.
Pariser, Fania, 22, 23.
Partition, 100, 137.
Peace Conference, at Versailles, 111, 115, 151.
Persitz Shosana, 105.
Petach Tikva, 30, 33, 90.
Petograd Conference, 109.
Pines, Yehiel Michal, 44, 45.
Pinsker, Dr. J. L., 31, 45, 87, 141, 147, 149.
Plehve, Count, 55, 56, 57.
Practical Zionism, 48, 66, 81.

Poale-Zion, 88.
Political Zionism, 47, 48, 49, 71, 80, 81, 93, 147.

Rehavia, 147.
Rehovoth, 90.
Riots of May, 1921, 115.
Rishon-le-Zion, 34, 69, 90, 119.
Rosenbaum, S., 68.
Rothschild, Baron (the Baron), 33, 52, 61, 69, 129.
Round Table Conference, 143.
Royal (Peel) Commision, 138.
Ruppin, Dr. Arthur, 90, 122, 123.
Russian Government, 88, 103.
  Pogrom, 19.
  Revolution of 1905, 81, 85, 86.
  Revolution of February, 1917, 107, 109.
  Socialists, 19.
  Zionism, Zionists, 48, 49, 56.

Safa Berura, 44.
San Remo, 121.
Samaria, 129.
Samuel, Sir Herbert, 116, 117, 125, 130.
Schapira, Prof. Herman, 23, 96, 135.
Schulman, Kalman, 18, 66.
Schatz, Prof. Boris, 96.
Sefer Ussishkin, 36, 94, 141, 146.
Sefatenu Itanu, 44.
Sfog (pseudonym of Samuel Tchernowitz), 69.
Sharon Plain, Valley, 129, 133.
Shephelah, cities of the, 144.
Shomer Hatzair, 145.
Sifriat Agura, 44.
Simeon bar Giora, 39.

Smaller Zionist Actions Committee, 60, 83.
Smolenskin, Peretz ben Moshe, 18.
"Socialist Zionist," 68, 83, 88, 118.
Society for Immigration to the Land of Israel, 21, 22.
Sokolow, Nahum, 27, 69, 111, 149.
Spiro, André, 111.
Spiritual Zionism, 44, 48, 50.
Storrs, Sir Ronald, 116, 136.
Sultan, see Abdul Hamid.

Tachkemoni School, 90.
Tchernichowsky, Saul, 140, 150.
Tchlenow, Yehiel, 20, 26, 28.
Tel Aviv, 118, 130, 140, 143.
  Gymnasium, 107.
Teachers (Hebrew) Association, 150, 151.
  Central Committee, 91, 100.
  Federation, 61, 63.
Territorialism, 71, 72, 82, 83.
Tiomkin, Zeev (Vladimir), 43, 133.
The Tribune, 104.
Trumpeldor, Joseph, 104..
Turkey, 27, 43, 56, 61, 103, 110.
Turkish Government, 48, 69, 96.
  Constitution, 93.
Tushia Library, 44.
Touroff, Prof. Nisan, 137.
Tzalalichin, Yehuda, 23.

Uganda, 57, 61, 66, 67, 68, 70, 73, 82, 83, 85.
  Commission, 70.
  Conflict, 71, 124.
Ugandism, 72, 76.

United States, 21.
University of Jerusalem, see Hebrew University.
Ussishkin, Menahem, activities on Board of the Hebrew University, 103; activities in Ekaterinoslav district, 43, 50, 85, 86; at the Eight Conference of the *Hovevei Zion*, 101; attitude on Partition of Palestine, 100, 137, 140; Bar-Mitzva, 16, 17, 23; Cultural activities, 27, 28, 29, 35, 36, 40, 43, 44, 80, 85, 90-92, 96, 99, 100, 105, 117, 134, 137, 150; education, 15-18, 21, 25, 26, 33, 152; head of Jewish National Fund, 124, 127, 128, 134, 142, 148, 151, 152; *Hovevei Zion*, 25, 29, 35, 47, 86-98, 101, 108, 109; Language conflict, 100; marriage, 36; relation to Jerusalem, 35-45, 95, 99, 100; settling in Palestine, 115-119; visit to Palestine, 36-41, 57-63, 94-97, 99; visit to U.S.A., 124, 128.
Ussishkin, Moshe (Moses), Zvi, 15, 16, 17, 152.
Ussishkin, Reiza, 15.
Ussishkin, Samuel, 140.

Valley of Jehoshophat, 39.
Versailles Conference, see Peace Conference.
Vienna, 47, 57, 71, 135.
Volozhin Yeshivah, 16, 30, 62.

Wadi Hawareth, 138.
Wailing Wall, 37, 38, 39, 96, 139, 151.

Washington Conference of Jewish National Fund, 128.
Weizmann, Dr. Chaim, 101, 112, 122, 125, 135, 137, 149.
Wilhelm, II, Kaiser of Germany, 56.
Wolfson, David, 71.
World War first, 54, 99, 103, 113, 118, 127.
Second, 138.

Yatzkan, Samuel, Jacob, 69.
Yavetz, Z., 44.
Yellin, Prof. David, 44, 136.
Yeshivoth, 34, 80.
Yesod Hamaaleh, 33, 119.
Yevzerev, Yehuda Zvi, 28.
Yiddish, Yiddishists, Yiddishism, 91, 92, 104, 105, 107, 108, 137.
Yohannan of Gush Halav, 39.
Young Turks, 93, 94.
Yishuv, 28, 30, 34, 36, 48, 57, 58, 59, 60, 61, 77, 105, 106, 109, 116, 117, 137.

Zangwill, Israel, 82.
Zeire Zion, 88.
Zemach, S., 140.
Zichron Jacob, 58, 59, 60, 62, 69.
Convention, 59.
Zionei Zion, 70, 72, 82, 88.
Zion Mule Corps, see Jewish Legion.
Zionist Bank, see A.P.C.
Zionist Executive, 82, 99, 106, 139, 143.
Zlatopolsky, Hillel, 91, 105.